D0282747

The National Trust Book of
SORBETS, FLUMMERIES AND FOOLS

PURE ICE AT A

MOMENT'S NOTICE
BY THE
'CHAMPION' HAND ICE MACHINE
: SIMPLE, CERTAIN, & DURABLE.
NO EXPENSIVE FREEZING POWDERS.
Will make Ice Cream, Block Ice, Cool Wines,
&c.   Prices from £8 8s.   Ask for List F2.

SOLE LICENSEES—
PULSOMETER ENGINEERING CO., LTD
Nine Elms Ironworks, London, S.W.

The National Trust Book of

SORBETS
FLUMMERIES
AND FOOLS

COLIN COOPER ENGLISH

DAVID & CHARLES

Newton Abbot   London   North Pomfret (Vt)

(*facing title page*) An early ice cream machine, c1891
(*Mansell Collection*)

The jacket photograph is by courtesy of Lyons Maid.

British Library Cataloguing in Publication Data

English, Colin Cooper
    The National Trust book of sorbets, flummeries
    and fools.
    1. Desserts   2. Cookery (Cold dishes)
    I. Title
    641.8'6   TX773

    ISBN 0-7153-8609-3

© The National Trust 1985

All rights reserved. No part of this
publication may be reproduced, stored
in a retrieval system, or transmitted,
in any form or by any means, electronic,
mechanical, photocopying, recording or
otherwise, without the prior permission
of David & Charles (Publishers) Limited

Typeset by Typesetters (Birmingham) Ltd,
Smethwick, West Midlands
and printed in Great Britain
by Redwood Burn Limited,
Trowbridge, Wilts
for David & Charles (Publishers) Limited
Brunel House   Newton Abbot   Devon

Published in the United States of America
by David & Charles Inc
North Pomfret   Vermont 05053   USA

❧ CONTENTS ❧

⤑ ACKNOWLEDGEMENTS ⤐

I wish to thank the following for giving me a great deal of help during research for this book.

From the UK: Birds Eye Wall's Ltd, Lyons Maid, J. Lyons & Co Ltd, Margaret Donovan, Margaret Fry, the Bishop of Carlisle, The Ice Cream Federation, the Rev Canon R. J. W. Bevan of Carlisle Cathedral, and Jean Norton of Rookery Hall, Worleston, Nr Nantwich, Cheshire, for her unusual paw paw sorbet recipe.

From the USA: The American Dairy Association, Rosemont, Illinois, and the RCW Manufacturing Corporation, Danville, Virginia.

The author and publishers would like to express their gratitude to Janet Clarke for her kind help and advice.

⤳QUANTITIES AND CONVERSIONS⤳

The recipes in this book are written in imperial measure, with the approximate metric equivalents given in brackets, eg 1½pt (855ml) water. The metric equivalent will be rounded up or down to the nearest 5g or 5ml. For practical cookery purposes, plus or minus 5g or 5ml will make no difference. However, as the equivalents are not exact, it is most important to stay with one set of measurements and not use a mixture of both for the same dish.

Weight: 1oz=28.35g (rounded up to 30g)
8oz=226.8g (rounded down to 225g)
1lb=453.6g (rounded down to 450g)

Liquid: ¼pt=142.5ml (rounded down to 140ml)
½pt=285ml
1pt=570ml

1tsp=5ml
1tbsp=15ml

For American readers: 1pt=2½ US cups. The imperial pint is 20fl oz whereas the US pint is 16fl oz.

Unless stated otherwise, all eggs used in the following recipes are Class A, Size 2 (in old-fashioned language 'large').

ABBREVIATIONS USED IN THIS BOOK

oz = ounce   ml = millilitre
lb = pound   tsp = teaspoon
g = gram   tbsp = tablespoon
kg = kilogram

To my three sons –
Anthony, Alistair and Andrew
who all have a sweet tooth

⪼ INTRODUCTION ⪻

There is an infinite variety of 'ice creams', but they nearly all derive from four basic preparations – ice cream, water ice, iced mousse and parfait.

Ice cream is a frozen combination of milk, eggs (or custard), sweetening and flavouring. The basic vanilla ice cream mixture forms the base of many different desserts: some fruit ice creams, liqueur ice creams and all manner of speciality frozen desserts such as iced Swiss roll, ice cream gâteaux, iced vacherin, biscuits glacés, cassata, sundaes, coupes, iced charlottes, Baked Alaska and so forth.

Water ices are a combination of fruits or liquor, water and a sweetener. Direct derivations are sherbets (in the USA), sorbets, spooms, marquises and granités.

Iced mousses are made by combining an Italian meringue mixture with a flavouring and whipped cream. An iced mousse is, perhaps, the most elegant member of the ice cream family.

A parfait is an extremely delicate preparation, being a mixture of sugar syrup, egg yolks or whole eggs, whipped cream and a flavouring. Unlike other ice creams, the parfait and the iced mousse are never churned in an ice cream machine. They may be served just on their own but are more frequently used for iced soufflés and bombes.

There are now various ice cream machines on the market, ranging from inexpensive models which fit inside the deep freeze, to free-standing ones which have their own built-in refrigeration system and cost thousands of pounds. The ice cream machine used in these recipes is a middle of the range type, having a fibreglass outer bucket and an inner thin metal drum which revolves round a stationary paddle, thus keeping the ice cream or sorbet continually on the move. It is necessary to use alternate layers of ice and salt. Water freezes at 32°F (0°C), but milk and cream will not freeze until they are down to 20°F (−6.7°C). The salt melts the ice and produces a brine with a temperature around 17°F (−8.3°C), and it is this freezing brine which provides the refrigeration.

The advantage of using a machine is that the ice cream is lighter and smoother, and as more air is incorporated into the mixture, more portions are obtained – which for a family is very useful! The main disadvantage is that of cost, beginning with the initial purchase. Even though the outer churn may be of fibreglass, the inner thin metal drum (if not of stainless steel) will eventually rust and have to be renewed. The electric motor will eventually wear out (under heavy use) and need either rewinding or replacing. The other disadvantage is that a supply of ice and salt is required. The ice must be broken up into smallish pieces and set in layers round the thin metal drum: ice, salt, ice, salt and so on. As the act of churning is noisy, with the ice pieces crunching one against the other, I have found that if the machine can be placed in a room (scullery, utility room, etc) by itself, this is much kinder to the ear!

It should be emphasised that equally good ice creams and sorbets can be made without using an ice cream machine – it is purely a matter of choice. However, if the mixture for freezing is placed in the ice compartment of a refrigerator or in the deep freeze, the mixture remains static, so must be periodically removed and thoroughly beaten, both to break up ice crystals and to increase the volume of the mixture. In general, mixtures frozen in this way will not be as light as those prepared in an ice cream machine.

A sugar syrup is a simple solution of sugar in water, with the addition of lemon rind and juice. These syrups form the basis of all the fruit ice creams, water ices, sherbets and sorbets, and all their derivatives. The sugar density of the syrup (a measurement of the amount of sugar present) is very important. Sugar is an antifreeze, so the more there is in the syrup, the less likely it is to freeze. Too little sugar, and the mixture will freeze hard and not be at all palatable. The density must always be measured when the syrup is cold – not hot – for the mixture becomes denser upon cooling (up to 3 or 4 degrees of difference). It is measured by a specially designed instrument called a saccharometer, which is a glass or plastic tube weighted at the bottom end and graduated at the top. When the saccharometer is put into the syrup, it sinks until the level of the syrup matches a graduated reading. The denser the syrup, the higher the saccharometer will ride in it, and the higher will be the reading; the lower the density, the lower the reading.

The recipes in this book using sugar syrups have been carefully worked out so that a saccharometer will not be necessary. However, as cookery is not an exact science, each recipe is merely a good working guide. By slightly varying the stated amount of each ingredient, different results will be obtained. As a cookery student many years ago, I found that the most important word in cookery is 'Why?'. Asking persistent questions and experimenting lets you begin to understand cookery.

The most labour-saving way of making fruit ice creams or sorbets is always to keep a supply of cold syrup in the refrigerator; it is then only necessary to freeze this mixture with whatever flavouring is required. If using an ice cream machine, it is best to make several ice creams or sorbets one after the other, so that the ice left over from the first sorbet can be reused for the second one.

A sugar thermometer is a most useful (and not too expensive) addition to the kitchen equipment. It is graduated, showing the various levels of heat required for sugar boiling. As regards this book, its use will bring within range desserts such as parfaits, iced mousses, and Italian meringue. These thermometers can be bought from most good ironmongers and hardware stores.

Some frozen desserts may need a stabiliser such as gelatine to hold them together if they are to be kept for some time before consumption. A wine sorbet, for example, will tend to separate if kept for longer than two weeks, but the addition of a little gelatine will prevent this. Care must be taken when using gelatine to be as sparing as possible, as too much could alter the texture of the mixture. Stabilisers should not be necessary when the desserts are eaten as soon as they are made.

There are now commercial packet sorbet and ice cream mixes on the market. Sadly, for the most part these products bear little resemblance to the real article. A cook who uses them, perhaps seduced by the ease of adding powder to water at very low cost, is forgetting that no such confection can rival the delicious flavour obtained from using proper, natural ingredients. Moreover, in the case of sorbets, a packet mix can actually turn out to be more expensive than fresh ingredients. Packet sorbets are designed to remain on a supermarket shelf for an indefinite length of time, as close scrutiny of the list of ingredients will reveal, thus no fresh albumen (egg white) will be included. As egg white has the property of increasing the volume of a sorbet, the packet mix will probably remain heavy and synthetic.

Most ice creams kept in a freezer will need a short period of 'ripening' in the main compartment of a refrigerator before serving. This allows the ice cream time to soften sufficiently to be easy to serve, and lets the flavour be more pronounced. An average ripening time for a plastic container holding 2pt (1 litre) of ice cream will be about 30 minutes.

The way to create these delicious confections is to follow the recipes at first, until you are thoroughly familiar with them. Then, when you no longer need to look at the recipes, you can branch out and start experimenting with new flavours. To produce an original flavoured ice cream or sorbet that nobody has ever tasted before is really exciting!

⟫ ICE CREAMS ⟪

Nobody really knows exactly when the idea of freezing a dessert began, but legend has it that the Chinese, some 3,000 years ago, were making iced drinks by chilling fruit juices with snow. Certainly at the time of Confucius (500BC) there were accounts of ice cellars, where ice was stored in the winter. Alexander the Great (356–323BC) is said to have enjoyed a mixture of frozen honey, fruit juices and milk. However, the onerous task of obtaining the coolant necessary for this dish fell to his slaves, who were sent in relays to the mountains to gather up snow and ice. Nero Claudius Caesar, Emperor of Rome (AD54–68) made the same demands upon his slaves!

Marco Polo, having spent twenty-three years in China in various capacities, returned to Venice in 1292, bringing with him the recipe for ice cream – and so it entered Europe, as a special summer delicacy. Its introduction to France is attributed to Catherine de Medici, who came to France in 1533 to marry the king's son, Henri de Valois – later to become Henri II. With her she brought a retinue of Italian cooks, and soon French chefs were learning the art of ice cream making. Her son (later Henri III) is said to have eaten ice

creams every day. About this time, a new breakthrough had been made in Florence. Bernardo Buantalenti had found that the temperature of ice was lowered by the addition of salt. This helped the freezing process a great deal.

The stories of how ice cream first came to England are legion, and the truth is difficult to establish. One story is that Henrietta Maria, who arrived in England in 1625 to marry Charles I, was closely followed by a certain Gerrard Tissain, a French chef noted for his skills with ice creams. He invented a new sort of ice cream which pleased the king so much that he did not want anyone else to know about it and granted the chef a pension of £20 per annum to keep the secret safe. However, upon the king's execution, the chef thought himself freed from his promise. He returned to France, where he sold his secret recipe to the Café Napolitain in Paris, and so the famous Neapolitan ice creams came into being. Another story is that Jacques, a French chef to the Court of Charles I, created a cream ice which swiftly became a favourite dessert for nobility. It is certainly true that a dessert was named after this famous chef – Coupe Jacques – but whichever story is correct, Charles I, who liked his food, undoubtedly enjoyed ice creams as well.

The establishment serving the finest food tends to catch the public's attention, and in the seventeenth century, the Café Procope in Paris became the first to offer water ices to the ordinary man. So successful was it that the idea soon spread to other cafés and restaurants. Recipes for ice cream began to appear in cookery books. *The Experienced English Housekeeper* by Elizabeth Raffald, 1769, and *The New and Complete Confectioner*, 1750, both include them. Whole books on ice cream, though, came much later. In 1830 *The Art of Ice Cream Making* (possibly the first complete technical treatise on the subject) was written by Frederick Goetz, a German confectioner. By 1883 the first American book on the subject, *Ice Cream and Cakes*, had been published.

The introduction of ice creams to America is equally obscure. In 1708 a guest of Governor Bladen of Maryland stated: '. . . we had a dessert no less curious; among the rarities of which it was composed was some fine Ice Cream which, with Strawberries and Milk, ate most deliciously.' Many American presidents have enjoyed ice cream, and certainly George Washington, Thomas Jefferson and James Madison appreciated it. Dolly (President Madison's wife) is on record as having served strawberry ice cream at the White House at her husband's second inaugural ball in 1812 (using cream from the Madison dairy at Montpelier and strawberries from her own garden).

Ice cream eating had, by now, become an established summertime habit amongst the well-to-do, but was still totally dependent on natural ice for the freezing process and on servants to make it by hand. The old way of ice cream production (called the 'pot freezer' method) was both time-consuming and costly. The ingredients were placed in a thin drum, which was then sunk into a larger container or bucket containing the ice and salt mixture. A lid was put on and the contents then had to be kept moving by bodily rocking the bucket (interspersed with stirring) to make sure that freezing took place evenly.

By the nineteenth century, 'ice-harvesting' had become common in America, so ice was more readily available for ice cream production. Street vending had begun in New York, and in 1828 the *National Advertiser* reported that 'I Scream, Ice Cream' had been added to the varied collection of New York City street cries. However, in 1846 there came another major breakthrough. An American lady Nancy Johnson, invented the hand-cranked freezing machine. She introduced a paddle or 'dasher' into the drum thus enabling the mixture to be churned without moving the bucket, and this greatly speeded up the process. For some reason, Nancy Johnson did not patent her idea, and on 30 May 1848, William G. Young registered it with the patent office. So important was this new invention that within a few years there were many imitations on the market, and many new patents had been taken out.

In 1851, with improved machinery, an American milk dealer, Jacob Fussell, began wholesale ice cream manufacture in Baltimore, later opening factories in Boston, Washington and New York.

Mechanical refrigeration became possible in 1878, and batch freezers appeared in 1914. Today, ice cream is produced by continuous freezing of the mix in a non-stop flow.

For the story of ice cream as we know it in England, the starting point is 1860. At that time it was still only the affluent who could enjoy ice cream. However, Carlo Gatti came over to England from Italy, bringing his hand freezer with him. He started to peddle ice cream from his brightly coloured cart, and did well. Eventually he brought more workers over to England. They froze their ice cream mixture in the early morning and peddled it on their rounds during the day. Their cry 'Gelati, ecco un poco' ('Ices, have some') soon became 'hokey pokey' – a name which stuck and thus entered the everyday English language of the day.

In 1922 Thomas Wall was looking for a product to give employment to his staff in the summer months – when sales of pies and sausages were normally low because of the superstition that it was unsafe to eat pork products unless there was an 'R' in the month. The new product decided upon was ice cream. American mass-production methods were first studied, then production began on a very small scale, the idea being that the ice cream could be sold in the butchers' and fishmongers' shops already supplied by Wall's.

However, the butchers and fishmongers had other ideas – they only wanted to sell Wall's meat products, not the new revolutionary ice cream! Wall's now had a problem: they had a small workforce making the ice cream but no sales outlets. Fred Wall (Thomas Wall's brother) then hit on the idea of selling ice cream from a tricycle. One was purchased for £6, loaded with ice and ice cream brickettes, and a rider set off round the streets of Acton on the 16 July 1922. Sales were made and proved a great success, so a further nine tricycles were purchased in September of that year and soon the Wall's tricycle and its slogan 'Stop Me and Buy One' were to become very famous. By 1939 there were 8,500 of them operating from 136 depots up and down the country.

The other leading manufacturer, Lyons Maid, began business in 1925 as the ice cream department of its parent company, J. Lyons & Co Ltd. The first products to be made were a small range of bricks and choc ices, mostly for Lyons teashops. However, with the introduction of mechanical refrigeration, distribution was extended to confectionery and grocery shops throughout the United Kingdom. Then, in 1934, the company began selling its ice cream to cinemas and theatres.

In World War II, the production of ice cream was suspended when all edible oils and fats were needed to honour the food rations. Although peace came in 1945 (and with it the lifting of the ban), growth was severely restricted for some seven years because of the shortage of raw materials. During this time, the large firms rationed all of their customers, unlike some of the newer companies who let a smaller number of customers have as much as they wished. The result of this policy was that when ingredients became plentiful again, the large companies still had many customers and so had a much larger business potential. Unfortunately, some of the smaller companies went out of business because their share of the market was too small.

In the 1950s, when the austerity of food rationing ended, many new ice cream products were introduced. For instance, the American forces at bases such as Sealand and Greenham Common demanded dairy ice cream and also ice creams containing real fruit and liqueurs. So these were produced, the dairy ice cream being made with saltless butter. However, machines to put fruit into dairy ice cream were not then available in Britain, so American machines had to be imported. Ice cream gâteaux began to be in demand for Easter and Christmas.

And so, with many new products coming on the market and home refrigeration readily available, the public began to eat ice cream all the year round. Hotels and restaurants featured it regularly on menus, and retailers happily stocked it. Today, thirty years on, ice cream can be enjoyed by everyone. The Americans eat more of it than anyone else, but, nevertheless, we in Britain still manage to consume a staggering 5 billion portions of ice cream every year.

PATENT ICE BREAKER.

No. 3, Price £3 each.

Will take a piece of ice about 5 inches by 6 inches by 8 inches, breaking it into pieces about the size of chestnuts.

No. 4, Price £1. 10s. each.

Will take a piece of ice about 4 inches by 4 inches by 6 inches, and breaks it into very small pieces.

ICE PRICKERS.

FOUR-PRONGED ICE BREAKER.

Ice creams are divided into two basic groups: those with a milk base, and those with a syrup base.

MILK-BASED ICE CREAM
Each of the three vanilla ice cream recipes makes about 2pt (1 litre) and serves 8-10.

Vanilla Ice Cream (*made with eggs – method 1*)
Vanilla ice cream made with eggs is much more refined than ice cream made without them. However, it requires a great deal of care to make properly and the ice cream is more expensive, but when freshly made, it is utterly delicious!

1pt (570ml) milk	8oz (225g) caster sugar
1 vanilla pod or 3 drops vanilla	¼pt (140ml) whipping or
essence	double cream
6 egg yolks	

Put the milk to heat with the vanilla pod or vanilla essence in a heavy-bottomed saucepan. Beat the egg yolks with the sugar in a bowl until light and frothy; an electric mixer is ideal for this. When the milk boils, remove the vanilla pod and keep for re-use. Pour the boiling milk slowly on to the egg yolk and sugar mixture, and whisk for a few seconds to combine all the ingredients. Return to a slow heat and stir with a spatula until the mixture thickens, but do not let it boil or the eggs will curdle. For the test, remove the spatula from the mixture and run your finger along its back. If a clear line is left, the mixture is ready. Remove it from the heat and immediately strain into a cold bowl, and stir again. The hot custard coming into contact with the cold bowl has the effect of stopping any further cooking. When the custard is cold, whip the cream until stiff and fold it into the custard, then freeze it in the ice compartment of a refrigerator, or a freezer. After 1 hour, remove and beat thoroughly. Repeat until the mixture begins to harden into ice cream. The process takes about 4–5 hours.

Vanilla Ice Cream (*made with eggs – method 2 – ice cream machine*)
The ingredients are the same as for method 1, but the cream is added to the milk before the milk is heated. Follow method 1 to prepare the custard. When the custard is cold, pour it into the

freezing churn. Place the paddle and top in position, then put the freezing churn in the outer bucket. Connect up the motor. Pack chipped ice and rock salt around the freezing churn three-quarters of the way up (1 part rock salt to 6 of ice). Switch on. After about 30–45 minutes, the machine may well start to labour, indicating that the ice cream has started hardening. Switch off the motor. (Most modern motors have an automatic cut out so that the machine switches itself off to avoid damage.) Remove the ice cream from the freezing churn, place in a sealed container and set to finish hardening in a freezer.

Variations:
For a firmer ice cream reduce the sugar content; for a softer one, increase the sugar content; for a drier one reduce both the sugar content and egg yolks. (In contrast to English and European recipes for vanilla ice cream, those in North America tend to include a tiny amount of salt amongst the ingredients. It is purely a matter of taste.)

Vanilla Ice Cream (*made without eggs*)
A very acceptable ice cream can be made using custard powder in place of eggs and it is, of course, much easier and cheaper to make. Like the first recipe, it can form the basis of many other ice creams.

1oz (30g) custard powder	1 vanilla pod or 3 drops vanilla
1pt (570ml) milk	essence
8oz (225g) caster sugar	¼pt (140ml) whipping or
	double cream

Mix the custard powder with a little of the milk. Bring the remaining milk and sugar to the boil with the vanilla pod or vanilla essence. Add the custard powder/milk mixture. Stir, bring back to the boil and allow to simmer for 3 minutes. Strain the custard into a cold container (to stop further cooking) and let it cool. Whip the cream until stiff and fold into the custard. Freeze it in the ice compartment of a refrigerator, or a freezer. After 1 hour, remove and beat thoroughly. Repeat until the mixture begins to harden into ice cream. The process takes about 4–5 hours.

(*Ice cream machine*: Add the cream to the milk before heating. Prepare the custard following the recipe. Freeze as for a vanilla ice cream made with eggs, method 2. The ice cream will be ready in about 30–45 minutes.)

Each of these vanilla ice cream recipes is suitable for making any milk-based ice cream.

Caramel Ice Cream (*serves 8–10*)

For this recipe the quantities of sugar are altered slightly, as caramel forms the main flavouring.

2pt (1 litre) vanilla ice cream   1tbsp (15ml) water
3½oz (100g) caster sugar

Prepare a vanilla ice cream, but use only 5oz (140g) of sugar. Let it cool.

To make the caramel, place the sugar in a heavy-bottomed saucepan and heat slowly to the caramel stage. Great care must be taken with sugar at this heat (356°F, 180°C) as a sugar burn is very nasty indeed. Once the caramel stage has been reached, the cooking must be stopped as soon as possible; this is done by adding water. Water added to sugar at such a heat is instantly turned to steam, so only add a few drops at a time; this will be sufficient to reduce the sugar temperature and stop the cooking. Stir carefully with a wooden spatula, then add the remainder of the water. It is not necessary to add anything else to the saucepan. Leave to cool, then blend in with the ice cream mix and set to freeze as for a vanilla ice cream.

Chestnut Ice Cream (*serves 8–10*)

2pt (1 litre) vanilla ice cream   3tbsp (45ml) Maraschino
9oz (255g) chestnuts

Use either fresh, peeled chestnuts cooked in milk with a drop of vanilla essence, or the tinned variety. If whole, purée them in a liquidiser. Add the Maraschino. Blend with the vanilla ice cream mix, and set to freeze as for a vanilla ice cream.

Chocolate Ice Cream (*serves 8–10*)

3½oz (100g) Menier (or similar fine quality) chocolate   7oz (200g) caster sugar
1tbsp (15ml) hot sorbet syrup (see page 32)   1 vanilla pod or 3 drops vanilla essence
1oz (30g) custard powder   ¼pt (140ml) whipping or double cream
1pt (570ml) milk

Break the chocolate into small pieces, and gently heat in a double boiler, or a bowl over a pan of hot water, together with 1tbsp (15ml) hot sorbet syrup. Stir the chocolate until it is all melted. Mix the custard powder with a little milk. Bring the remaining milk, sugar and vanilla pod or vanilla essence to the boil. Remove the vanilla pod, then add the chocolate and the custard powder/milk mixture. Stir, bring back to the boil, then simmer for 3 minutes. Strain the custard into a cold container (to stop further cooking) and let it cool. Whip the cream until stiff and fold into the custard. Freeze as for vanilla ice cream.

Variation:
Chocolate Mint Ice Cream
Add 6tbsp (90ml) chocolate peppermint liqueur or Crème de Menthe to the chocolate ice cream mixture before freezing takes place. When the ice cream begins to harden, remove from the freezer, and fold in 2oz (55g) grated Menier (or other fine quality) chocolate. Return to the freezer.

(*Ice cream machine*: Place the ice cream mixture in the churn without the grated chocolate. When the ice cream has solidified, remove from the churn and fold in the grated chocolate. Leave to harden in the freezer. If the chocolate is added beforehand, it will tend to break up into very small pieces and spoil the look of the finished ice cream.)

Chocolate Fudge Ice Cream (*serves 8–10*)

1½pt (855ml) milk	4oz (115g) Menier (or similar
4oz (115g) caster sugar	fine quality) plain chocolate
8 egg yolks	¼pt (140ml) whipping or
1 vanilla pod or 3 drops	double cream
vanilla essence	
6oz (170g) home-made (or	
bought) fudge	

As the chocolate and fudge contain quite a lot of sugar, the amount of further sugar in the recipe must be limited (otherwise the ice cream will not freeze). Make a vanilla ice cream with only 4oz (115g) sugar, and 1pt (570ml) milk. Melt the fudge and chocolate in the remaining ½pt (285ml) milk, then blend into the vanilla ice cream mixture. Whip the cream until stiff. Set to freeze as for a vanilla ice cream.

The process takes about 4–5 hours (or about 30–45 minutes in an ice cream machine). Serve this ice cream with hot chocolate fudge sauce (see page 000).

21

Rich Chocolate Rum Ice Cream (*serves 6–8*)

This is made very quickly, but is extremely rich and definitely not for those on a diet!

6oz (170g) Menier (or similar fine quality) plain chocolate
8fl oz (230ml) condensed milk

2tbsp (30ml) Jamaican rum.
½pt (285ml) whipping or double cream

Break the chocolate into small pieces, place in a pan with the condensed milk and heat gently. Stir slowly and when the chocolate has melted, remove from the heat and leave to cool. When cold, add the rum. Whip the cream until stiff and fold into the chocolate mixture. Blend well and set to freeze. The process will take about 4–5 hours.

(*Ice cream machine:* Place the mixture with the cream into the churn. Set to freeze. The ice cream will be ready in about 30–45 minutes.)

Coffee Ice Cream (*serves 8–10*)

2pt (1 litre) vanilla ice cream   4tbsp (60ml) coffee essence

Whilst preparing the vanilla ice cream, add the coffee essence to the milk. Freeze as for a vanilla ice cream.

Liqueur Ice Cream (*serves 8–10*)

Virtually any liqueur can be added such as Maraschino, Grand Marnier, kirsch, Cointreau, Strega, Drambuie, etc.

2pt (1 litre) vanilla ice cream   6tbsp (90ml) liqueur

When making the vanilla ice cream, add the liqueur before freezing starts. Freeze as for a vanilla ice cream.

Pistachio Ice Cream (*serves 8–10*)

2pt (1 litre) vanilla ice cream   1–2 drops green food colouring
5oz (140g) pistachio nuts   (optional)

Blanch the nuts and remove their skins. Grind the nuts into a powder in a food processor or liquidiser. Blend with the vanilla ice cream mix, adding the green colouring (if used). Freeze as for a vanilla ice cream.

Praline Ice Cream (*serves 8–10*)

2pt (1 litre) vanilla ice cream   7oz (200g) praline (see page 87)

Prepare a vanilla ice cream using only 5oz (140g) caster sugar for 1½pt (855ml) milk. This is to balance the sugar in the praline. Grind the praline to a fine powder and add to the vanilla ice cream mix. Freeze as for a vanilla ice cream.

Rum and Raisin Ice Cream (*serves 8–10*)

2pt (1 litre) vanilla ice cream   6tbsp (90ml) rum
4oz (115g) washed raisins

Soak the raisins in the rum for 1 hour. Strain. When making the vanilla ice cream, add the rum before freezing starts. Freeze as for a vanilla ice cream. When the ice cream begins to harden, remove from the freezer and fold in the raisins. Return to the freezer.

(*Ice cream machine*: Place the ice cream in the churn, but add the rum before churning starts. When the churning is completed, remove the ice cream from the churn, fold in the raisins, and leave to harden in the freezer.)

Tea Ice Cream (*serves 8–10*)
This is an unusual but very refreshing ice cream.

1pt (570ml) milk   6 egg yolks
4tsp (20ml) Lapsang Souchong,   8oz (225g) caster sugar
   or Earl Grey tea   ¼pt (140ml) whipping or
1 vanilla pod or 3 drops vanilla   double cream
   essence

Bring the milk and tea gently to the boil. Remove and leave to infuse for 10 minutes. Strain, and prepare as for a vanilla ice cream.

Tutti-Frutti Ice Cream (*serves 8–10*)

2pt (1 litre) vanilla ice cream   5½oz (155g) mixed candied
                                                 peel, angelica and glacé
                                                 cherries

Set the vanilla ice cream to freeze in the normal way. Just before it has solidified, remove from the freezer and stir in the mixed candied peel, angelica and glacé cherries. Set to harden in the freezer.

(*Ice cream machine*: Place the ice cream in the churn and prepare in the normal way, without the mixed candied peel, etc (which would get trapped in the paddle as it churned). When the ice cream has solidified, remove from the churn and fold in the mixed candied peel, etc. Leave to harden in the freezer.)

Walnut and Tia Maria Ice Cream (*serves 8–10*)

2pt (1 litre) vanilla ice cream   4tbsp (60ml) Tia Maria
2tbsp (30ml) coffee essence   7oz (200g) shelled walnuts

When making the vanilla ice cream, add the coffee essence and Tia Maria before freezing starts. Freeze as for a vanilla ice cream. Partially crush the walnuts so that they remain a little chunky. When the ice cream begins to harden, remove from the freezer. Fold in the crushed walnuts and return to the freezer.

(*Ice cream machine*: Churn the ice cream without the walnuts. When the ice cream begins to solidify, add the walnuts and continue churning for 2–3 minutes. Remove the ice cream and leave to harden in the freezer.)

Variation:
Walnut and Honey Ice Cream
Substitute 4tbsp (60ml) runny honey for the Tia Maria.

SYRUP-BASED ICE CREAM

If fruit is merely added to a milk-based ice cream, the milk tends to mask its taste; the best flavour is obtained by using a sugar syrup and fruit purée. The addition of cream is optional, but I think it gives a smoother, richer result.

Ice Cream Syrup (*makes about 2pt [1 litre]*)

1¼pt (710ml) water
15oz (425g) granulated sugar

Juice and thinly pared rind of
  1 lemon
2 drops vanilla essence

Bring water and sugar to the boil in a heavy-bottomed pan. Whilst the mixture is heating up, add the thinly pared rind of the lemon. (Never just cut the lemon in two halves and add these, as the pith will make the syrup bitter.) Once at boiling point, leave the syrup to bubble for exactly 1 minute. Immediately remove from the heat, add the lemon juice and vanilla essence, then pour into a cold container and leave to cool. When cold, strain. Cover and store in the refrigerator, where it will keep for up to 2 weeks.

Banana Ice Cream (*serves 8–10*)

1pt (570ml) cold ice cream
  syrup
8–9 large bananas

Juice of 1 lemon
¼pt (140ml) whipping or
  double cream

Peel and liquidise the bananas with the lemon juice (thus stopping the discoloration of the bananas). Add to the syrup straight away and set to freeze. After 1 hour, remove, whip the cream until stiff and fold into the ice cream mixture. Beat thoroughly. Replace in the freezer. Repeat until the mixture begins to harden into ice cream. The process takes about 4–5 hours.

(*Ice cream machine*: Combine the syrup, banana purée, lemon juice and cream. Freeze in the churn. The ice cream will be ready in about 30–45 minutes. Remove the ice cream, and leave to harden in the freezer.)

Variation:
Banana and Praline Ice Cream
The flavour of nuts and banana go well together. Reduce the amount of sugar in the ice cream syrup by 3½oz (100g). Add 3½oz (100g) praline (see page 87) to the banana and ice cream syrup mixture. Freeze as for a banana ice cream.

Blackberry Ice Cream (*serves 8–10*)

2pt (1 litre) hot ice cream syrup Juice of 1 lemon
3 × 12oz (340g) packs frozen   ¼pt (140ml) whipping or
  (or fresh) blackberries   double cream

Make the ice cream syrup according to the recipe. As soon as it has
finished boiling, add the frozen (or fresh) blackberries and lemon
juice. Liquidise, then rub through a fine sieve, so that any pips are
removed. When completely cold, set to freeze. After 1 hour,
remove, whip the cream until stiff and fold into the ice cream
mixture. Beat thoroughly. Replace in the freezer. Repeat until the
mixture begins to harden into ice cream. The process takes about
4–5 hours.
 (*Ice cream machine*: Combine the syrup, blackberries and lemon
juice. Liquidise the mixture and rub through a fine sieve. Add the
cream. Freeze in the churn. The ice cream will be ready in about
30–45 minutes. Remove the ice cream and leave to harden in the
freezer.)

Blackcurrant Ice Cream (*serves 8–10*)

2pt (1 litre) cold ice cream syrup Juice of 1 lemon
3 × 12oz (340g) packs   ¼pt (140ml) whipping or
  blackcurrants   double cream

Liquidise the blackcurrants with a little of the syrup. Rub through a
fine sieve and add to the rest of the syrup, together with the lemon
juice. Set to freeze. After 1 hour, remove, whip the cream until stiff
and fold into the ice cream mixture. Beat thoroughly. Replace in the
freezer. Repeat until the mixture begins to harden into ice cream.
The process takes about 4–5 hours.
 (*Ice cream machine*: Liquidise the blackcurrants with a little of
the syrup. Rub through a fine sieve. Combine the syrup, blackcurrant purée, lemon juice and cream. Freeze in the churn. The ice
cream will be ready in about 30–45 minutes. Remove the ice cream
and leave to harden in the freezer.)

Variation:
Redcurrant Ice Cream
Substitute redcurrants for blackcurrants. You may need 1–2 drops
of red food colouring.

Damson Ice Cream (serves 8–10)

2pt (1 litre) hot ice cream syrup   ¼pt (140ml) whipping or
1lb 5oz (600g) damsons   double cream

Poach the damsons in the syrup for about 10 minutes until the fruit is soft. Leave to cool overnight. When cold, strain, remove the stones and liquidise the pulp to a fine purée. Set to freeze. After 1 hour, remove, whip the cream until stiff and add to the mixture. Repeat until the mixture hardens into ice cream. The process will take about 4–5 hours.

(*Ice cream machine*: Combine syrup, damson purée and cream. Freeze in churn. The ice cream will be ready in about 30–45 minutes.)

Variation:
Plum Ice Cream
Substitute plums for damsons.

Lemon Ice Cream (serves 8–10)
This is a very tangy and delicious ice cream.

2pt (1 litre) hot ice cream syrup   ¼pt (140ml) whipping or
Rind and juice of 8–10 large   double cream
  lemons

Make the ice cream syrup according to the recipe. Add the rind of all the lemons as the syrup heats up. After the syrup has been taken off the heat, add the strained lemon juice. When the syrup is cold, strain. Set to freeze. After 1 hour, remove, whip the cream until stiff and fold into the ice cream mixture. Beat thoroughly. Repeat until the mixture begins to harden into ice cream. The process takes about 4–5 hours (or about 30–45 minutes if using an ice cream machine).

If the freezing takes place in the ice cream compartment of a refrigerator or freezer, it might be best to leave out the cream, as it could curdle with the lemon juice. If the freezing takes place in an ice cream machine, there is no problem, and cream can be used very effectively.

Variation:
Orange Ice Cream
Substitute oranges for lemons, but still add the juice of 1 lemon for every 2pt (1 litre) mixture. You may need a drop of red food colouring.

Mango Ice Cream (*serves 4–6*)

For those not familiar with the colour of mangoes, the finished ice cream is a most beautiful shade of orange.

1pt (570ml) cold ice cream syrup
2 ripe mangoes

⅛pt (70ml) whipping or double cream

Skin the mangoes and remove all the flesh from the long, flat stone. Liquidise the flesh. Add to the syrup and set to freeze. After 1 hour, remove, whip the cream until stiff and fold into the ice cream mixture. Beat thoroughly. Replace in the freezer. Repeat until the mixture hardens into ice cream.

(*Ice cream machine*: Combine the syrup, mango purée and cream. Freeze in the churn. The ice cream will be ready in about 30–45 minutes. Remove the ice cream and leave to harden in the freezer.)

Melon Ice Cream (*serves 6–8*)

1pt (570ml) cold ice cream syrup
1 ripe Honeydew melon (size 5 – see page 37)
Juice of 1 lemon

Juice of 1 small orange
1–2 drops green food colouring (optional)
¼pt (140ml) whipping or double cream

Discard the melon peel and pips. Liquidise the flesh. Combine the syrup with the purée, then add the juice of the lemon and orange, and the green colouring (if used). Set to freeze. After 1 hour, remove, whip the cream until stiff and fold into the ice cream mixture. Beat thoroughly. Replace in the freezer. Repeat until the mixture begins to harden into ice cream. The process takes about 4–5 hours.

(*Ice cream machine*: Combine the syrup, melon purée, lemon and orange juice, cream and colouring (if used). Freeze in the churn. The ice cream will be ready in about 30–45 minutes. Remove the ice cream and leave to harden in the freezer.)

Peach Ice Cream (*serves 6–8*)

1pt (570ml) cold ice cream
  syrup
1pt (570ml) fresh or tinned
  peaches

¼pt (140ml) whipping or
  double cream

If using tinned peaches, drain thoroughly and liquidise the peaches (keep the juice for a fruit sorbet). If using fresh peaches, first remove their skins by plunging the fruit into boiling water for 10 seconds, then liquidise them. Combine the syrup with the purée. Set to freeze. After 1 hour, remove, whip the cream until stiff and fold into the ice cream mixture. Beat thoroughly. Replace in the freezer. Repeat until the mixture begins to harden into ice cream.

(*Ice cream machine*: Combine the syrup, peach purée and cream, and freeze in the churn. The ice cream will be ready in about 30–45 minutes. Remove the ice cream and leave to harden in the freezer.)

Variations:
Apricot Ice Cream
Substitute apricots for the peaches.

Mixed Fruit Ice Cream
Substitute mixed fruit for the peaches.

Pineapple Ice Cream (*serves 8–10*)

2pt (1 litre) cold ice cream syrup
2 × 1½lb (680g) fresh
  pineapples
Juice of 1 lemon

¼pt (140ml) whipping or
  double cream

Remove thick outer skin and inner core from the pineapples. Liquidise the flesh. Combine the syrup with the purée, add the lemon juice, and set to freeze. After 1 hour, remove, whip the cream until stiff and add to the mixture beating thoroughly. Replace in the freezer. Repeat until the mixture begins to harden into ice cream. The process takes about 4–5 hours.

(*Ice cream machine*: Combine syrup, pineapple purée, lemon juice and cream, and freeze in churn. The ice cream will be ready in about 30–45 minutes.)

Variation:
Pineapple and Kirsch Ice Cream
Add 1tbsp (15ml) kirsch to the mixture before freezing begins. This is a delicious ice cream.

Raspberry Ice Cream (*serves 8–10*)

2pt (1 litre) hot ice cream syrup
3×12oz (340g) packs fresh or frozen raspberries
Juice of 1 lemon
¼pt (140ml) whipping or double cream

Make an ice cream syrup according to the recipe. As soon as it has finished boiling, add the raspberries and lemon juice. Liquidise, then rub the purée through a fine sieve, so that any pips are removed. When completely cold, set to freeze. After 1 hour, remove, whip the cream until stiff and fold into the ice cream mixture. Beat thoroughly. Replace in the freezer. Repeat until the mixture begins to harden into ice cream.

(*Ice cream machine*: Liquidise the raspberries with a little of the syrup. Rub through a fine sieve. Combine syrup, raspberry purée, lemon juice and cream. Freeze in the churn. The ice cream will be ready in about 30–45 minutes. Remove ice cream and leave to harden in the freezer.)

Strawberry Ice Cream (*serves 6–8*)

1pt (570ml) cold ice cream syrup
1pt (570ml) fresh or tinned strawberries
1–2 drops red food colouring (optional)
Juice of 1 lemon
¼pt (140ml) whipping or double cream

Liquidise the strawberries and rub the purée through a fine sieve to remove any pips. Combine the syrup with the purée. Add the red colouring (if used) and the lemon juice. Set to freeze. After 1 hour, remove, whip the cream until stiff and fold into the ice cream mixture. Beat thoroughly. Replace in the freezer. Repeat until the mixture begins to harden into ice cream.

(*Ice cream machine*: Liquidise the strawberries with a little of the syrup. Rub through a fine sieve. Combine syrup, strawberry purée, lemon juice, cream, and colouring (if used). Freeze in churn. The ice cream will be ready in about 30–45 minutes. Remove ice cream and leave to harden in the freezer.

Note: Strawberries adapt quite well to being blended with vanilla ice cream. However, the milk does tend to neutralise the natural strawberry flavour.

≫ SORBETS ≪

Unfortunately, the word sorbet (derived from the Arabic *sharbah*, meaning drink) is very misleading nowadays. A true sorbet is a water ice with the addition of egg whites and sugar in the form of Italian meringue. A sherbet is the accepted American term for a water ice (or sorbet) and is sometimes made with a milk base; it may or may not have added meringue. The product which most of us consumed as children – sherbet powder – is a mixture of tartaric acid, bicarbonate of soda and sugar, plus different flavourings. The derivations of sorbets, such as spooms, granités and marquises, are described in later chapters.

Sorbets are frequently served between the entrée and roast courses of formal meals, for a light ice at this point cleanses the palate before the highlight of the meal is served. These sorbets are usually made from a wine, such as champagne, or a liqueur. Nowadays, however, with more people interested in a lighter diet, sorbets are increasingly being served as a sweet.

Virtually all sorbets benefit from the addition of a liqueur or brandy, and the recipes include these details. They are, of course, optional.

As regards the meringue, I have found that if icing sugar is used rather than caster sugar, a smoother result is obtained, and it is much easier to prepare than the more lengthy Italian meringue. The recipes, therefore, use icing sugar in uncooked meringue; however, if Italian meringue is desired, just substitute caster for icing sugar (see following methods).

Sorbet Syrup (*makes about 1pt [570ml]*)

¾pt (425ml) water   Rind and juice of 1 lemon
7oz (200g) granulated sugar

Bring the water and sugar to the boil in a heavy-bottomed pan. Whilst the mixture is heating up, add the rind of the lemon. (Never just cut the lemon in two halves and add these, as the pith will make the syrup bitter.) Once at boiling point, leave the syrup to bubble for 1 minute. Immediately remove from the heat and add the lemon juice, then pour into a cold container and leave to cool. When cold, this syrup will last for about a week if kept in the refrigerator, and can be used for most sweet sorbets.

The reason for less sugar being present in this syrup than the ice cream one is to allow for the addition of the sugar in the meringue.

Italian Meringue (*cooked*)

8oz (225g) granulated sugar   4 egg whites
¼pt (140ml) water

Heat the sugar and water together in a heavy-bottomed pan. Check the temperature with a sugar thermometer. Whilst the sugar is heating up, whisk the egg whites until stiff. When the sugar temperature reaches soft-ball stage (about 240°F/115°C), remove the thermometer, taking care to let it cool slowly on a warm surface, and pour the hot syrup in a thin thread on to the egg whites whilst continuing the whisking. When all the syrup has been absorbed, continue whisking until the mixture is cold. This meringue can be used straight away, or will keep, covered with a damp cloth, for several days in the refrigerator.

Meringue (*uncooked*)

4 egg whites   8oz (225g) icing sugar

Whisk the egg whites until very stiff, but not dry. Thoroughly sift the icing sugar and gradually fold it into the egg whites. This mixture will only keep for a day and is best used immediately.

Champagne Sorbet (*serves 10–12*)
This procedure is the basis, in general, for all sorbets.

1pt (570ml) cold sorbet syrup   2 egg whites
1pt (570ml) champagne   4oz (115g) icing sugar

Blend the champagne and sorbet syrup, and set to freeze. After every hour, remove from the freezer and beat the mixture thoroughly. This will help to break up any large ice crystals and also beat in some air. Repeat this process until the mixture starts to go opaque and hardens. Replace in the freezer. Whisk the egg whites until stiff, then fold in the well-sifted icing sugar. Add this mixture to the sorbet, remembering that the meringue gives a sorbet its lightness. Replace in the freezer. Leave for a further 2 hours, beating well every half hour. To make a sorbet in this way in the freezing compartment of a refrigerator of freezer will take about 4–5 hours.

As an alternative, pink champagne gives a delightful colour to the sorbet. Any sparkling wine can be used in this way, even fizzy cider, but it will not be a champagne sorbet!

(*Ice cream machine*: Place the sorbet mixture in the freezing churn, replace the paddle and top, then place in the outer bucket. Connect up the motor. Pack chipped ice and rock salt around the freezing churn three-quarters of the way up (1 part salt to 6 of ice). Switch on. After about 30 minutes, the machine may well start to labour, indicating that the sorbet has started hardening. Switch off the motor. Incidentally, most modern motors have an automatic cut out so that the machine switches itself off to avoid damage. Prepare the meringue. Fold this mixture into the sorbet, then replace the paddle, top and motor, and switch on again. As the meringue and sorbet cool they stiffen and incorporate air into the mixture, thus rendering it very light indeed. When the mixture is fairly stiff (a further 15 minutes should suffice), remove it from the drum, place in a sealed container and set to finish hardening in the deep freeze.)

If this sorbet (or any non-fruit-pulp sorbet) is to be kept for a period longer than 2 weeks, it may be necessary to use gelatine as a stabiliser. Some wine or citrus-based sorbets have a tendency to separate if kept for a long time in the freezer. Unfortunately, this will not work very well if the sorbet is made in the freezing compartment of a refrigerator or freezer, because the gelatine will set unevenly, making the sorbet slightly rubbery in places. In an ice cream machine, the paddles keep the sorbet on the move all the time, thus the gelatine is evenly distributed throughout the sorbet.

If gelatine is to be used, allow ½oz (15g) gelatine per 2pt (1 litre) sorbet mixture. Heat 2tbsp (30ml) cold sorbet syrup. Sprinkle the gelatine on to the hot syrup and let it melt. Pass through a strainer into the sorbet mixture, and freeze in the normal way.

Apple and Cider Sorbet (*serves 10–12*)

1pt (570ml) cold sorbet syrup	2tbsp (30ml) Calvados
½pt (285ml) apple juice	2 egg whites
½pt (285ml) sweet cider	4oz (115g) icing sugar

Blend all the ingredients except the egg whites and icing sugar. Freeze as for a champagne sorbet, adding the meringue when the sorbet hardens.

Banana Sorbet (*serves 6–8*)

1pt (570ml) cold sorbet syrup	2tbsp (30ml) Crème de Banane
4–6 large bananas	2 egg whites
Juice of 1 lemon	4oz (115g) icing sugar

Peel and liquidise the bananas together with the lemon juice and liqueur. Blend with the cold syrup. Freeze as for a champagne sorbet, adding the meringue when the sorbet hardens.

Blackcurrant Sorbet (*serves 10–12*)

3×12oz (340g) punnets of blackcurrants	Juice and rind of 1 lemon
1pt (570ml) water	2tbsp (30ml) Crème de Cassis
10½oz (300g) granulated sugar	2 egg whites
	4oz (115g) icing sugar

Top, tail and thoroughly wash the blackcurrants. Bring the water, sugar, blackcurrants and lemon rind to the boil in a heavy-bottomed pan. Once at boiling point, simmer for 2–3 minutes until the blackcurrants are tender. Remove from the heat, strain, and rub the fruit through a fine sieve. Leave to cool. Add the lemon juice and Crème de Cassis. Freeze as for a champagne sorbet, adding the meringue when the sorbet hardens.

Variations:
Redcurrant Sorbet
Substitute 3×12oz (340g) redcurrants for the blackcurrants. Do not add Crème de Cassis. You may need 1–2 drops of red food colouring.

Blackcurrant and Rum Sorbet
Substitute 2tbsp (30ml) rum in place of the Crème de Cassis.

Coffee Sorbet (*serves 6–8*)

1pt (570ml) cold sorbet syrup	2 egg whites
1pt (570ml) water	4oz (115g) icing sugar
2tbsp (30ml) coffee essence	

Boil the water, pour over the coffee essence and leave to cool. Combine with the syrup. Freeze as for a champagne sorbet, adding the meringue when the sorbet hardens.

Variation:
Coffee and Tia Maria Sorbet
Add 2tbsp (30ml) Tia Maria to the coffee mixture before freezing the sorbet.

Cola and White Rum Sorbet (*serves 6–8*)
I devised this sorbet during the long dry summer of 1984. It is based on the delicious Spanish drink 'Cuba Libre' – a combination of Cola and white rum.

1pt (570ml) water	2tbsp (30ml) white rum
Rind and juice of 1 lemon	2 egg whites
9oz (255g) granulated sugar	4oz (115g) icing sugar
1pt (570ml) fizzy or still cola	

Boil the water with the lemon rind and sugar. Boil for 1 minute, then strain and allow to cool. Add the cola, rum and lemon juice. When completely cold, freeze as for a champagne sorbet, adding the meringue when the sorbet hardens.

Damson Sorbet (*serves 12–15*)
This has a delightful, very rich plum colour. Try serving it with a white sorbet, such as lemon; the colour contrast is most effective.

1lb 5oz (600g) damsons	4tbsp (60ml) damson wine
2pt (1 litre) water	(optional)
1lb (450g) granulated sugar	4 egg whites
Rind and juice of 1 lemon	8oz (225g) icing sugar

Poach the damsons in the water with the sugar and lemon rind for about 10 minutes until the damsons are soft. Strain the mixture, remove the stones and liquidise so that the skins and flesh are reduced to a very fine pulp. Leave to cool overnight. Add the lemon juice and damson wine (if used). Freeze as for a champagne sorbet, adding the meringue when the sorbet hardens.

Grapefruit and Crème de Menthe Sorbet (*serves 6–8*)

1pt (570ml) cold sorbet syrup	2tbsp (30ml) Crème de Menthe
4 large grapefruits	2 egg whites
½pt (285ml) grapefruit juice	4oz (115g) icing sugar

Carefully remove the grapefruit flesh from the skins (these can be used for serving the sorbet in, if desired). Separate the segments and liquidise, blending them with the grapefruit juice, cold sorbet syrup, and Crème de Menthe. Freeze as for a champagne sorbet, adding the meringue when the sorbet hardens.

Lemon Sorbet (*serves 6–8*)

1pt (570ml) cold sorbet syrup	2 egg whites
8 large lemons	4oz (115g) icing sugar

Squeeze the juice from the lemons, and grate the rind from 2 of them. Blend with the cold sorbet syrup, and freeze as for a champagne sorbet, adding the meringue when the sorbet hardens.

(*Ice cream machine*: Although this is a most delicious sorbet, lemon juice is very acidic and will attack the metal of the churn if it is not made of stainless steel. The mixture must therefore be removed from the churn as soon as possible after the completion of churning.)

Variations:
Lemon and Lime Sorbet
Substitute 6 limes for half of the lemons; use the grated rind of 1 lemon and 1 lime. Make the sorbet in exactly the same way. This is a delicious alternative.

Orange Sorbet
Substitute oranges for the lemons. Make the sorbet in exactly the same way. Add Cointreau or Grand Marnier.

Lemon Milk Sherbet (*serves 10–12*)
Maple syrup can be used in place of corn syrup, but it is very expensive. Full cream milk is best for this sherbet; if skimmed milk is used, the flavour will not be as good.

2 egg whites	1pt (570ml) milk
4oz (115g) icing sugar	Grated rind of 1 lemon
½pt (285ml) corn syrup	Juice of 6 lemons

Whisk the egg whites until stiff, then gradually fold in the sugar. Blend the corn syrup, milk, lemon rind and juice together, and add to the meringue mixture. Freeze as for a champagne sorbet.

Melon Sorbet (*serves 6–8*)
Honeydew melons are usually graded by size according to the number in a box. Thus 14s are 14 to a box, 5s are 5 to the box, and so on. The pulp from a size 5 melon, which is about the average size, yields approximately 1pt (570ml) juice when liquidised.

This particular sorbet is a rarity – a true sorbet that can be successfully served as a starter or as an intermediate course in a large meal, as well as a sweet.

1pt (570ml) cold sorbet syrup	2 egg whites
1 ripe Honeydew melon (size 5)	4oz (115g) icing sugar
1tbsp (15ml) kirsch	

Discard the melon peel and pips. Liquidise the flesh. Combine the sorbet syrup with the purée and kirsch. Freeze as for a champagne sorbet, adding the meringue when the sorbet hardens.

Mint Sorbet (*serves 10–12*)
This is a most refreshing sorbet, especially if served on a hot evening in the summer. Garnish with fresh mint leaves.

2pt (1 litre) hot sorbet syrup	2tbsp (30ml) Crème de Menthe
4 good handfuls fresh mint leaves	2 egg whites
2–3 drops green food colouring (optional)	4oz (115g) icing sugar

Strip and wash the mint leaves. Make the sorbet syrup according to the recipe. As soon as it has come to the boil, add the mint leaves and boil for exactly 1 minute, then remove from the heat, leaving the mint to steep in the syrup until cool. Then strain the syrup through a sieve and add the Crème de Menthe and green colouring (if used). When completely cold, freeze as for a champagne sorbet, adding the meringue when the sorbet hardens.

Variation:
Chocolate Mint Sorbet
Make a mint sorbet. When it starts to harden, remove from the freezer. Grate 2oz (55g) Menier (or other fine quality) chocolate and fold into the sorbet. Return to the freezer.

Mixed Fruit Sorbet (*serves 6–8*)

This is an excellent sorbet for the summer, when possibly some fruit salad is left over, or you are looking for a means of using up small amounts of fruit.

1pt (570ml) cold sorbet syrup   2 egg whites
1pt (570ml) mixed fruit purée   4oz (115g) icing sugar
2tbsp (30ml) kirsch

Blend all the ingredients except the egg whites and icing sugar. Freeze as for a champagne sorbet, adding the meringue when the sorbet hardens.

Note: If using grapes in this sorbet, make sure that the skins are either removed or properly liquidised. They tend to spoil the look of the sorbet if left in pieces.

Paw Paw Sorbet (*serves 4–6*)

Apart from being most colourful and delicious, the paw paw has another bonus. It is extremely digestible, containing an enzyme which is now used commercially in tenderising meat.

½pt (285ml) cold sorbet syrup   Juice of half a lemon
4 paw paw fruits   5 egg whites

Peel and pip the paw paw. Cut into strips and leave in a bowl overnight sprinkled with the lemon juice. Put in a blender with a little of the syrup and blend until very smooth. Mix with the rest of the syrup and freeze as for a champagne sorbet. Adjust lemon juice to taste before adding the whisked egg whites.

Note: Ripe paw paw is very sweet – the lemon juice helps to counteract this – hence there is no meringue added, merely egg whites without sugar.

Peach Sorbet (*serves 6–8*)

1pt (570ml) cold sorbet syrup	2tbsp (30ml) peach brandy
1pt (570ml) fresh or tinned peaches	2 egg whites
	4oz (115g) icing sugar

Skin and destone the peaches (blanch fresh peaches in boiling water for 10 seconds to loosen the skins). Liquidise the flesh and blend with the cold syrup and peach brandy. Freeze as for a champagne sorbet, adding the meringue when the sorbet hardens.

Variation:
Apricot Sorbet
Substitute apricots for peaches, and apricot brandy for peach brandy. Make the sorbet in exactly the same way.

Raspberry Sorbet (*serves 12–15*)
Eau-de-Vie de Framboises is an extraordinarily fragrant raspberry liqueur, so very little is needed to perfume the sorbet. It is, unfortunately, also difficult to obtain and expensive.

1pt (570ml) cold sorbet syrup	1tbsp (15ml) Eau-de-Vie de
2 × 12oz (340g) punnets fresh or thawed frozen raspberries	Framboises (optional)
	2 egg whites
	4oz (115g) icing sugar

Liquidise the raspberries and rub the purée through a fine sieve to remove the pips. Blend with the syrup and liqueur (if used). Freeze as for a champagne sorbet, adding the meringue when the sorbet hardens.

Red Wine Sorbet (*serves 10–12*)

1pt (570ml) cold sorbet syrup	2 egg whites
1pt (570ml) Beaujolais, Rioja or claret (or red wine of choice)	4oz (115g) icing sugar

Combine red wine with the syrup. Set to freeze as for a champagne sorbet, adding the meringue when the sorbet begins to harden.

Variation:
Rosé Wine Sorbet
Substitute rosé wine for the red wine.

Satsuma Sherbet (*serves 6–8*)

This sherbet has no egg whites in it. It is, therefore, denser than a sorbet.

1½lb (680g) fresh satsumas   Juice of 1 orange
8oz (225g) caster sugar

Peel the satsumas, liquidise them, then rub them through a fine sieve (as the membranes between each segment will still remain and spoil the finished sherbet). Add the pulp to the sugar and orange juice. Once the sugar has dissolved the mixture can be frozen. Freeze as for a champagne sorbet, omitting the meringue stage.

Strawberry Sorbet (*serves 10–12*)

1pt (570ml) cold sorbet syrup   1–2 drops red food colouring
1lb (450g) fresh or tinned   (optional)
  strawberries   2 egg whites
2tbsp (30ml) brandy   4oz (115g) icing sugar

Wash and hull the strawberries, then liquidise them. If tinned ones are used, liquidise the whole contents of the cans – strawberries and syrup. If you do not want the pips, rub the purée through a fine sieve. Blend with the cold syrup, brandy and the red colouring (if used). Freeze as for a champagne sorbet, adding the meringue when the sorbet hardens.

Tea Sorbet (*serves 10–12*)

This sorbet requires a fine, delicate-flavoured tea. Do not economise by using tea bags – they will not produce a good sorbet.

1pt (570ml) cold sorbet syrup   2 egg whites
1pt (570ml) water   4oz (115g) icing sugar
4tsp (20ml) Lapsang Souchong
  or Earl Grey tea

Bring the water to the boil and pour on to the tea leaves. Allow to infuse for 10 minutes, then strain and leave the tea to cool. Blend with the cold syrup. Freeze as for a champagne sorbet, adding the meringue when the sorbet hardens.

⫸ PARFAITS AND MOUSSES ⫷

Parfaits and iced mousses are extremely light and are the most delicate of all the frozen desserts. There is very little difference between the two except that, as a rule, parfaits contain egg yolks or whole eggs, whereas iced mousses are made from an Italian meringue base and so use just the egg whites. Both these preparations form the base for iced soufflés and bombes; they also take longer to freeze than other ice creams, needing a full 5 hours in the freezer before being ready to serve.

PARFAITS
The original flavour for a parfait was coffee. Nowadays any suitable flavouring can be used, though not every recipe is suitable for every flavouring. There are, therefore, several basic recipes. The recipes for parfaits and iced mousses each make about 2pt (1 litre) mixture.

Iced Coffee Parfait (*serves 6*)

3½oz (100g) caster sugar	2tbsp (30ml) coffee essence
2tbsp (30ml) water	½pt (285ml) whipping or
4 egg yolks	double cream

Heat the sugar and water, together with a sugar thermometer, in a heavy-bottomed pan. When the temperature reaches 240°F (115°C), carefully pour the syrup in a very thin thread on to the yolks, then whisk them over heat until they begin to thicken and become like a mousse. Remove from the heat and continue to whisk until cold (this can be done over crushed ice if you prefer). Add the coffee essence to the cream and whip until stiff. Using a wooden spoon, fold the cream very carefully into the egg and sugar mixture. Set to freeze.

Variations:
Iced Chocolate Parfait
Substitute 1oz (30g) cocoa powder for the coffee essence.

41

Iced Chocolate Peppermint Parfait
As above, but add 1 or 2 drops peppermint essence to taste.

Iced Kirsch Parfait (*serves* 6)
This recipe is slightly different from the iced pistachio parfait that
follows in that the amount of egg white is reduced, being replaced
by white wine, in order to make the flavour of the liqueur more
prominent. This recipe is, therefore, best used for all the liqueur-
based parfaits. Almost any liqueur can be used in this recipe.

4 egg yolks
1 whole egg
4oz (115g) caster sugar
1tbsp (15ml) sweet white wine

2tbsp (30ml) kirsch
½pt (285ml) whipping or
  double cream

Combine the egg yolks and whole egg with the sugar and wine.
Whisk over heat until the mixture thickens like a mousse. Remove
from the heat and continue whisking until the mixture is cold (this
is quickest done over crushed ice). Add the kirsch to the cream and
whip until the cream is stiff. Carefully fold into the parfait mixture.
Set to freeze.

Iced Pistachio Parfait (*serves* 6)

3 egg yolks
3 whole eggs
5oz (140g) caster sugar
4oz (115g) blanched pistachio
  nuts

½pt (285ml) whipping or
  double cream
A drop of green food colouring
  (optional)

Whisk the yolks and whole eggs with the sugar over heat in a
double boiler, or a bowl over a pan of hot water. When the mixture
thickens, becoming like a mousse, remove from the heat and continue whisking until cold (this is quickest done over crushed ice).
Pound the nuts (in either a mortar and pestle or a food processor).
Whip the cream until stiff, add the pounded nuts and then carefully
fold this into the egg and sugar mixture, together with the green
colouring (if used). Set to freeze.

Variation:
Iced Praline Parfait
As above, but substitute 2oz (55g) granulated sugar and 2oz (55g)
blanched almonds (cooked into a praline mixture – see page 87) for
the pistachio nuts.

MOUSSES

Iced Grand Marnier Mousse (*serves 6–8*)

4½oz (125g) granulated sugar	2tbsp (30ml) Grand Marnier
4tbsp (60ml) water	½pt (285ml) whipping or
3 egg whites	double cream

Boil the sugar with the water. Meanwhile, whisk the egg whites until stiff. When the syrup reaches 240°F (115°C) on the sugar thermometer, remove from the heat, and immediately pour it carefully in a thin thread on to the whisked egg whites. Continue whisking until cold. Add the Grand Marnier to the cream and whip until stiff, then gently fold into the meringue mixture. Set to freeze, which will take about 5 hours.

Variation:
Using this recipe, all iced mousses of liqueurs, coffee, chocolate, etc, can be made.

Iced Praline Mousse (*serves 6–8*)
For this dish, less sugar is required for the meringue, to allow for sugar in the praline.

1½oz (45g) caster sugar	4tbsp (60ml) water
1½oz (45g) flaked almonds	½pt (285ml) whipping or
3 egg whites	double cream
3oz (85g) granulated sugar	

Using the caster sugar and flaked almonds, make a praline mixture (see page 87). Whisk the egg whites until stiff. Boil the granulated sugar with the water. When the syrup reaches 240°F (115°C) on the sugar thermometer, remove from the heat, and immediately pour it carefully in a thin thread on to the egg whites. Continue whisking until cold. Add the praline to the cream and whip until stiff. Gently fold this into the meringue. Set to freeze, which will take about 5 hours.

Iced Raspberry Mousse (*serves 6–8*)

6oz (170g) granulated sugar
2fl oz (55ml) water
3 egg whites
9oz (255g) raspberries
1 small lemon

1tbsp (15ml) Eau-de-Vie de
   Framboises (optional)
½pt (285ml) whipping or
   double cream

Boil the sugar with the water. Meanwhile whisk the egg whites until stiff. When the syrup reaches 240°F (115°C) on the sugar thermometer, remove from the heat, and immediately pour it carefully in a thin thread on to the egg whites. Continue whisking until cold. Liquidise the raspberries and rub them through a fine sieve to remove the pips. Add a few drops of lemon juice and the liqueur (if used). Whip the cream until peaks form, then gently fold the cream and fruit pulp into the meringue. Set to freeze, which will take about 5 hours.

Variations:
Using this recipe, substitute any fruit with a pulp base, ie non-citrus.

The following mousses are not frozen.

Apricot Mousse (*serves 4–6*)

8oz (225g) tinned apricots
   (chilled)
3 eggs
4oz (115g) caster sugar
Juice of half a lemon
1tbsp (15ml) water
½oz (15g) gelatine

¼pt (140ml) whipping or
   double cream
TO DECORATE:
A little whipping or
   double cream
Toasted flaked almonds

The day before they are required, chill the apricots. For the recipe, thoroughly drain the apricots and liquidise them. Whisk the eggs and sugar together until thick and moussy; the mixture should be stiff enough to form peaks. Gently heat the lemon juice and water together, and dissolve the gelatine in this, but be careful not to let it boil. Whip the cream. Fold the apricot purée, cream and egg mousse mixture together. Quickly fold in the gelatine mixture. The chilled apricot purée will tend to make the gelatine start to set, so the mousse must be portioned out into attractive glasses as soon as possible. Leave to set in the refrigerator. Decorate with a simple rosette of whipped cream and some toasted almonds.

Chocolate, Brandy and Orange Mousse (*serves 4*)

4oz (115g) Menier (or similar fine quality) chocolate
Grated rind and juice of 1 orange
1tbsp (15ml) brandy
4 eggs

TO DECORATE:
A little whipping or double cream
Grated orange rind

Melt the chocolate with the orange juice, half the grated orange rind and the brandy over a low heat. Stir until all the chocolate has melted. Separate the eggs, beating the yolks a little in a mixing bowl. Pour the hot chocolate on to the yolks and continue beating so that the yolks cook slightly and thicken. Keep beating until the mixture cools, then whisk the whites until stiff and carefully fold them into the chocolate and yolks. Make sure that this mixture is well blended and uniform, as the egg whites tend to remain in lumps and the chocolate can sink. Pipe into individual glasses and chill. To decorate, whip the cream, pipe into rosettes on top of the mousses and sprinkle on the remaining grated orange rind.

Coffee and Maple Mousse (*serves 4–6*)

3 egg yolks
¼pt (140ml) maple syrup
2tsp (10ml) coffee essence or instant coffee
1tbsp (15ml) dark rum
½oz (15g) gelatine

¼pt (140ml) whipping or double cream

TO DECORATE:
Whipping or double cream
A few chopped walnuts

Whisk the egg yolks until frothy. Heat the maple syrup, coffee and rum in a double boiler or a bowl over a pan of hot water, until hot, but not boiling. Add the gelatine and stir until it has dissolved. Remove from the heat. Whilst still hot, pour in a thin thread on to the egg yolks and continue whisking so that they cook a little. Transfer to a cold bowl and leave to cool. Whip the cream until fairly stiff, then fold into the egg and syrup mixture. Portion into attractive glasses and leave to set in the refrigerator. Decorate each mousse with a rosette of whipped cream and sprinkle on the chopped walnuts.

Variation:
Coffee and Hazelnut Mousse
Prepare as above but add 2oz (55g) finely ground hazelnuts to the whipped cream. Decorate with a little praline (see page 87).

Drambuie Mousse (*serves 6–8*)

6 egg yolks
2oz (55g) caster sugar
4tbsp (60ml) Drambuie
2tbsp (30ml) lemon juice
2tbsp (30ml) orange juice

TO DECORATE:
¼pt (140ml) whipping
  or double cream
Caraque chocolate (see page 87)
  or toasted flaked almonds

Whisk the egg yolks, sugar, Drambuie and fruit juices in a double boiler or a bowl over a pan of hot water. When stiff and moussy, pour into individual tall-stemmed glasses and chill. When ready for serving, pipe a rosette of whipped cream on the top of each mousse. Decorate with toasted almonds or caraque chocolate.

Variation:
Cointreau Mousse
Substitute Cointreau (or any liqueur) for the Drambuie.

Lemon Mousse (*serves 4–6*)

3 eggs
4oz (115g) caster sugar
½oz (15g) gelatine
TO DECORATE:
Grated lemon rind

Juice of 4 large lemons
¼pt (140ml) whipping or
  double cream

Whisk the eggs and sugar until thick and moussy. Dissolve the gelatine in the lemon juice over a gentle heat. Whip the cream until stiff. Carefully blend the gelatine into the egg mixture, and fold in the cream. Portion into attractive glasses and leave to set in the refrigerator. As this sweet is already rich in cream, just add grated lemon rind as decoration.

Rum and Black Coffee Mousse (*serves 6–8*)

This is an extremely light, delicious mousse which is suitable for those not wanting a rich sweet. It is best eaten on the day it is made.

4tsp (20ml) coffee essence or instant coffee
9oz (255g) granulated sugar
1pt (570ml) water
1oz (30g) gelatine

4tbsp (60ml) rum
3 egg whites
¼pt (140ml) whipping or double cream

TO DECORATE:
Chopped walnuts

Add the coffee to the sugar and heat in the water until the sugar has dissolved – about 5 minutes. Add the gelatine and rum to the syrup whilst it is still hot and stir well. Set on one side to cool. When the mixture is almost cold and just before it starts to set, whip it briskly to incorporate air. Whisk the egg whites and cream separately until they are both stiff, then delicately fold them both into the rum and coffee syrup. Portion into attractive glasses and leave in the refrigerator to set. Decorate with the chopped walnuts.

Zabaglione (*serves 6–8*)

This dessert is also excellent when poured on to other hot sweets as a sauce.

12 egg yolks
14oz (395g) caster sugar
¼pt (140ml) Marsala wine

¼pt (140ml) whipping or double cream

TO DECORATE:
Thinly sliced rind of 1 lemon

Heat a pan of water on the stove with a glass bowl above it. Place the egg yolks, sugar and Marsala in the bowl and begin whisking. When the mixture becomes moussy and stiffer, pour it into a cold bowl, continuing to whisk until it cools. Whip the cream until stiff, and carefully fold this into the mixture. Portion into attractive glasses and leave to set in the refrigerator. Decorate with the thinly sliced lemon rind. This zabaglione will last for 2–3 days in the refrigerator.

Variations:
Any liqueur flavouring.

⇒ ICED SOUFFLÉS, ICED BOMBES ⇐ AND BISCUITS GLACÉS

ICED SOUFFLÉS

Soufflés take their name from the French verb *souffler*, meaning to blow. (In a hot soufflé, it is the air inside the mixture which expands on heating, so making the soufflé rise.) Iced soufflés are prepared using either a mousse or parfait mixture, and they are one of the most appreciated of cold sweets.

Iced Coffee Soufflé (*serves* 6)

3 egg yolks
3 whole eggs
5oz (140g) caster sugar
4tbsp (60ml) coffee essence

½pt (285ml) whipping or
  double cream
½oz (15g) cocoa powder (for
  decoration)

Cut a strip of greaseproof paper or Bakewell paper 3 × 23in (7.5 × 57.5cm). Smear a little butter on the two ends. Wrap the paper carefully round the top of a 7in (17.5cm) soufflé dish so that half the paper is below the rim and half is above. Press the edges together so that the butter sticks them, then tie the paper securely with string. The reason for this is so that the mixture can be filled above the level of the rim and will have the appearance of a cooked soufflé when served.

    Whisk the yolks and whole eggs with the sugar over heat in a double boiler or in a bowl over a pan of hot water. When the mixture starts to thicken and become moussy, remove from the heat and continue whisking until cold (this can be done over crushed ice, if you prefer). Add the coffee essence to the cream and whip until stiff. Carefully fold this into the egg and sugar mixture. Fill the soufflé dish to the top of the paper and set to freeze. This will take about 5 hours. When ready to be served, untie the string and remove the paper. Put the cocoa powder into a sieve and shake over the top of the iced soufflé. This, again, is to simulate a cooked soufflé in appearance.

Variations:
Iced Chocolate Soufflé
Substitute 3oz (85g) Menier (or similar fine quality) chocolate for the coffee essence. Freeze, and decorate as for an iced coffee soufflé.

Iced Cointreau Soufflé
Use the recipe for an iced kirsch parfait. Substitute Cointreau for the kirsch. Freeze (allowing up to 6 hours), and decorate as for an iced coffee soufflé.

Iced Noisette Soufflé
Substitute 7oz (200g) praline (see page 87) for the coffee essence. Freeze, and decorate as for an iced coffee soufflé.

Iced Strawberry Soufflé
Use the recipe for an iced raspberry mousse. Substitute strawberries for the raspberries. You may need a drop of red food colouring. Freeze, and decorate as for an iced coffee soufflé.

Iced Lemon Soufflé
Use the recipe for an Iced Grand Marnier Mousse. Substitute 2tbsp (30ml) lemon juice for the Grand Marnier. Add the lemon juice to the cream before whipping, then fold into the Italian Meringue mixture. Freeze, and decorate as for an iced coffee soufflé, perhaps adding some thinly sliced rind of lemon.

ICED BOMBES

Bombes are moulded iced puddings, so named because of their shape. They usually combine several flavours. One flavour is used to line the mould, and another to fill the inside of the bombe. Sometimes, fruits are added, and these are much better if chopped into small pieces and soaked for 2–3 hours in a liqueur. The variations of flavours are virtually unlimited.

Bombe Georgette (*serves 10–12*)

1pt (570ml) praline ice cream
2pt (1 litre) iced kirsch parfait
¼pt (140ml) whipping or
   double cream

1oz (30g) toasted flaked
   almonds

Bombe moulds are usually hemispherical, but expensive, so an excellent substitute is an ordinary 7in (17.5cm) plastic pudding bowl. Line this with greaseproof paper or Bakewell paper and set to chill in the freezer for 1 hour.

Cover the bottom and sides of the bowl with the praline ice cream. Return to the freezer for half an hour. When the ice cream has hardened again, remove the bowl from the freezer and fill the inside with the kirsch parfait. Cover the top with greaseproof paper or Bakewell paper and return to the freezer for 4 hours.

To serve, dip the bowl in warm water, remove the paper covering, turn the bowl upside down on to a serving dish and lift it off the bombe. Remove the paper lining. Whip the cream and pipe attractive rosettes along the base and top of the bombe. Sprinkle toasted flaked almonds on top of each cream rosette.

Variations:
Bombe Aida
Use tangerine ice for the lining and a kirsch mousse for the inside.

Bombe Alhambra
Use vanilla ice cream for the lining and strawberry mousse for the inside. Decorate with fresh strawberries soaked in kirsch and sprinkled with sifted icing sugar.

Bombe Ceylan
Use coffee ice cream for the lining and rum mousse for the inside.

Bombe Grimaldi
Use vanilla ice cream for the lining and kümmel mousse for the inside.

Bombe Josephine
Use coffee ice cream for the lining and pistachio mousse for the inside.

Bombe Marie Louise
Use chocolate ice cream for the lining and vanilla mousse for the inside.

Bombe Othello
Use praline ice cream for the lining and peach mousse for the inside.

Bombe Parisienne
Use raspberry ice cream for the lining and for the inside vanilla parfait together with 2oz (55g) cherries, destoned and roughly chopped, which have been previously soaked in 2tbsp (30ml) kirsch.

Bombe Coppélia
Use coffee ice cream for the lining and praline mousse for the inside.

Bombe Sicilienne
Use lemon ice cream for the lining and praline mousse for the inside.

Bombe Talleyrand
Use caramel ice cream for the lining and vanilla parfait for the inside. Add 2oz (55g) ratafias soaked in curaçao to the vanilla parfait when filling the inside of the bombe.

Bombe Tortoni
Use praline ice cream for the lining and rum-flavoured coffee parfait for the inside.

BISCUITS GLACÉS

These delicious French sweets generally have three distinct layers. The first is ice cream; the second is a thin layer of light Genoese sponge liberally soaked in a liqueur or syrup; and finally, there is a layer of iced mousse or parfait. They are served in thick slices. The art of preparing these desserts is to marry the flavours well, and the combinations are virtually unlimited. Sometimes, the sponge layer is omitted, being replaced by another flavour of ice cream. This is popularly known as a 'Neapolitan ice cream'. The French term *'biscuits'* in this instance, refers to the portions being cut into a rectangular shape – like a biscuit.

Biscuit Glacé Excelsior (*serves 8–10*)

9 × 5in (23 × 12.5cm) rectangular layer of Genoese sponge (see page 57)
1pt (570ml) vanilla ice cream

6tbsp (90ml) maraschino
2tbsp (30ml) cold sorbet syrup or ice cream syrup
1pt (570ml) pistachio ice cream

Line a 9 × 5in (23 × 12.5cm) rectangular loaf tin with either greaseproof paper or Bakewell paper. Cut the sponge so that it will fit the loaf tin, then, when it is the right size, put it on a small tray. Fill the bottom of the tin with a layer of vanilla ice cream. Replace in the freezer for half an hour to harden. Meanwhile, blend the maraschino and syrup, and soak the sponge. Remove the tin from the freezer and carefully place the sponge in position on top of the vanilla ice cream. Replace in the freezer for half an hour. Remove, and add the final layer – the pistachio ice cream. Cover with grease-proof paper or Bakewell paper and return to the freezer.

To serve, dip the loaf tin in warm water, remove the paper covering from the top, turn the loaf tin upside down on to a serving dish and lift if off the biscuit glacé. Cut in thick slices.

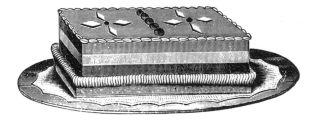

Variations:
Biscuit Glacé Antoinette
Use vanilla ice cream for the base, then a layer of sponge soaked with kirsch, and iced raspberry mousse for the top layer.

Biscuit Glacé Bresilien
This is really delicious. Use caramel ice cream for the base, then a layer of sponge soaked in rum, and praline mousse for the top layer.

Biscuit Glacé Mont Blanc
Use rum ice cream for the base, chestnut ice cream for the second layer (there is no sponge), and vanilla ice cream for the top layer.

Biscuit Glacé Napolitain
There are several variations to this. Use pistachio ice cream for the base, iced strawberry mousse for the second layer, and praline parfait for the top layer. Sometimes, vanilla ice cream is used for the top layer.

Biscuit Glacé Tortoni
Use pistachio ice cream for the base, then a layer of sponge soaked in maraschino, and iced strawberry mousse for the top layer.

⧉ SPECIALITY FROZEN DESSERTS ⧉

Baked Alaska (*serves 6–8*)
This dish is ideal when you have egg whites or sponge to use up.

9in (22.5cm) square sponge   4 egg whites
  cake   8oz (225g) caster sugar
1pt (570ml) vanilla ice cream

Make the sponge into a rectangle by cutting 2in (5cm) from two opposite sides. Slice these in half lengthwise. Scoop out the ice cream and shape it into a pyramid on the sponge base. Lay the thin slices of sponge on top of the ice cream so that it is completely covered. The layer of sponge acts as an insulator and stops the ice cream from melting in the oven. Place in the freezer for half an hour to harden up.

Set the oven to hot (425°F, 220°C, Gas Mark 7). Make the meringue and spread it evenly all over the sponge pyramid. Bake in the oven for 4–5 minutes. Remove from the oven and serve at once.

Variations:
Ruche Edouard VII
There are some similar French sweets called *ruches* (beehives). Almost the same as Baked Alaska, but use strawberry ice cream and add a dice of peaches. Decorate in the shape of a beehive and quickly brown in the oven. Serve at once.

Cassata (Basic Mixture)

6oz (170g) granulated sugar
2½fl oz (70ml) water
3 egg whites
1oz (30g) mixed glacé cherries
and angelica

2tbsp (30ml) maraschino or rum
3oz (85g) hazelnuts
¾pt (430ml) whipping or
double cream
3oz (85g) candied peel

Heat the sugar and water together in a heavy-bottomed pan. Check the temperature with a sugar thermometer. Whilst the sugar is heating up, whisk the egg whites until stiff. When the sugar temperature reaches soft-ball stage (240°F, 115°C), remove the thermometer (taking care to let it cool slowly on a warm surface) and pour the hot syrup in a thin thread on to the egg whites whilst continuing the whisking. When all the syrup has been absorbed, continue whisking until the mixture is cold.

Finely chop the glacé cherries and angelica, and soak them in the maraschino or rum. Toast the hazelnuts in the oven then grind them almost to a fine powder in a food processor or blender. Whip the cream until it is slightly thicker than required for normal piping (take care it does not turn to butter). Fold in the candied peel, glacé cherries, angelica and ground hazelnuts. Carefully fold in the Italian meringue. The cassata mixture is now complete.

Cassata Napolitain (*serves 12–14*)

Cassatas can be made in many different moulds. However, for home use the most practical is the rectangular loaf tin, as a cassata in this shape is very easy for cutting into portions when required.

¾pt (430ml) vanilla ice cream
¾pt (430ml) chocolate ice
cream

¾pt (430ml) strawberry ice
cream
Cassata mixture (see above)

Line the loaf tin 3in (7.5cm) by 9in (22.5cm) by 5in (12.5cm) with greaseproof paper or Bakewell paper and thoroughly chill it in the freezer. Line the tin with a ½in (1cm) layer of vanilla ice cream. Return to the freezer for half an hour. Then add the layer of chocolate ice cream to the same thickness. Return to the freezer for half an hour. Add the strawberry ice cream layer. Return to the freezer for half an hour. Fill with the cassata mixture. Cover with greaseproof paper or Bakewell paper and then with foil, and freeze for 4–5 hours.

To serve, remove from the freezer, and dip the loaf tin in warm water. Dry thoroughly, remove the foil and paper, then turn out the cassata on to a serving dish and remove the paper lining.

Cherries Jubilee (*serves 4–6*)

A dish often seen in restaurants, where it is flambéed at the table.

½pt (285ml) tinned, pitted
  black cherries
1oz (30g) butter
1oz (30g) granulated sugar
Rind and juice of half a lemon

Rind and juice of half an orange
2tbsp (30ml) kirsch
½pt (285ml) vanilla ice cream
2tbsp (30ml) brandy

Thoroughly drain the cherries. Melt the butter in a flambé pan (or small frying pan) over a high heat. Add the sugar when the butter starts to sizzle. Grate the lemon and orange into the pan and simmer until the mixture turns a light brown. Add the juice from both fruits, and leave to cook until the mixture starts to bubble again. Add the kirsch and cherries, and stir so that all the flavour of the sauce is absorbed by the cherries. Portion the ice cream into dessert dishes. Warm the brandy and add it to the sauce. Strike a match and light the brandy. Let the flames subside, then immediately pour the sauce over the ice cream and serve at once.

Iced Charlotte Royale (*serves 8–10*)

1 Swiss roll (see page 57)
2pt (1 litre) vanilla ice cream,
  not hardened

½pt (285ml) whipping or
  double cream
12–14 glacé cherries

Line an 8in (20cm) plastic pudding bowl with either greaseproof paper or Bakewell paper. Thinly slice the Swiss roll and, starting at the bottom, line the sides of the bowl with the slices till you reach the top. Fill with the vanilla ice cream. Freeze for 2–3 hours. When required, turn the charlotte upside down and remove the pudding bowl and lining paper. Whip the cream and, using a piping bag with a star-shaped nozzle, pipe little rosettes around the base and top of the charlotte. Decorate with the glacé cherries.

Variations:

Iced Charlotte Plombière

Substitute sponge fingers for the Swiss roll, and use tutti-frutti ice cream instead of vanilla ice cream.

Iced Rainbow Charlotte

Instead of one type of ice cream, use three or four – the more contrasting the colours and flavours, the better. Line the mould with thin slices of Swiss roll as for the iced charlotte royale. Gradually fill the inside with the different ice creams, layer by layer.

Iced Pineapple Punch (*serves 4–6*)

4oz (115g) icing sugar	½pt (285ml) cold ice cream
½pt (285ml) fresh or tinned	syrup
pineapple	¼pt (140ml) champagne
2 egg whites	2tbsp (30ml) kirsch

Thoroughly sift the icing sugar. Liquidise the pineapple into a purée. Whisk the egg whites till stiff, then carefully fold in the icing sugar. Mix all the remaining ingredients together and set to freeze. After 1 hour, remove and beat well, then add the meringue. The freezing takes about 3–4 hours (or about 30–45 minutes in an ice cream machine).

Iced Swiss Roll (*serves 6–8*)

This is a very practical sweet to make in advance and freeze. Most children love it – so it is very useful in school holidays!

4½oz (125g) plain flour	2–3tbsp (30–45ml) apricot jam
6 eggs	½pt (285ml) vanilla ice cream
4½oz (125g) caster sugar	or flavour of choice

Thoroughly sift the flour. Separate the egg yolks from the whites. Whisk the egg whites until stiff, then add half the sugar, little by little, until a smooth, shiny mixture is obtained. Beat the yolks together with the remaining half of the sugar until light and creamy. Quickly, with a wooden spatula, fold the egg white mixture into the yolk mousse, together with the sifted flour. This is what gives the sponge its lightness.

Spread the mixture to a depth of ⅓in (0.8cm) in a non-stick 8 × 12in (20 × 30cm) Swiss roll tin which is, in effect, a tray with shallow ½in (1cm) sides. If the Swiss roll tin is not non-stick, line it first with Bakewell paper. The amount of sponge mix in this recipe will fill three Swiss roll tins. Bake in a hot oven (400°F, 204°C, Gas Mark 6) for 8–10 minutes, until the surface of the sponge becomes firm and slightly golden.

Remove the sponge from the oven and turn it out on to a sheet of Bakewell paper well dredged with sugar. Leave to cool. Spread evenly with a thin layer of apricot jam, then the ice cream and, using the Bakewell paper, roll up the sponge into the familiar Swiss role shape. Trim the edges, cover with foil or transparent film, label and freeze.

Iced Tangerines (*serves 12*)

12 tangerines
1pt (570ml) cold ice cream
  syrup
Juice of 1 lemon

Juice of 1 small orange
¼pt (140ml) whipping or
  double cream

Cut a neat hole about 1½in (3.75cm) in the top of each tangerine. Keep the tops for decoration. Remove all the pulp from the tangerines very carefully, so as not to break the peel. Liquidise the pulp and strain through a fine sieve. Blend the tangerine juice with the cold syrup, lemon juice and orange juice. (Tangerines do not have a very pronounced flavour, so the orange juice is added to give a slight lift.) Set to freeze.

After 1 hour, remove, add the cream and thoroughly beat the mixture. Do the same after every hour. The mixture will be ready after 4–5 hours (or about 30–45 minutes if using an ice cream machine). Remove and spoon into the tangerine shells. Overfill them slightly, then replace the tangerine tops. Place in the freezer until required for serving.

Iced Vacherin (*serves 6–8*)

FOR THE VACHERIN SHELLS:
4 egg whites
8oz (225g) caster sugar
A little caster sugar for
  sprinkling

FOR THE FILLING:
1pt (570ml) vanilla ice cream
½pt (285ml) whipping or
  double cream
8 glacé cherries, cut in half
1oz (30g) toasted flaked
  almonds

Whisk the egg whites till they stand in peaks. Slowly whisk in half the sugar (if using a machine, have it on the slowest setting at this point). Gradually fold in the remaining half of the sugar by hand, using a spatula. If the sugar is added too fast, air is beaten out of the meringue and it becomes heavy and too compact.

Line two baking trays with sheets of Bakewell paper. Using a piping bag with a star-shaped nozzle, start at the centre of the baking tray and pipe the meringue clockwise into the shape of a catherine wheel. Each vacherin should be about 8in (20cm) in diameter. Sprinkle on a little caster sugar. Bake very slowly in a cool oven (248°F, 120°C, Gas Mark ¼) for 3–4 hours. Remove from the paper and store in an airtight container until required.

Put one vacherin on a round cake tray. Spread with a ½in (1cm) layer of vanilla ice cream. Lay the second vacherin on top and very lightly press down. Leave to harden in the deep freeze until required. To serve, spread with a thin layer of whipped cream and decorate with rosettes of cream, glacé cherries and toasted flaked almonds.

Variation:
Iced Chestnut Vacherin
Thoroughly beat 3oz (85g) chestnut purée, then add it to the cream before whipping. Finish off as for the Iced Vacherin.

Iced Zabaglione (*serves 4–6*)
This is unusual and very delicious.

2 whole eggs	4 egg yolks
4oz (115g) caster sugar	⅛pt (70ml) Marsala
2tbsp (30ml) water	

Separate the egg whites from the yolks. Whisk the egg whites until stiff, then make an Italian meringue by boiling the sugar and water till it reaches 240°F (115°C), and adding it in a thin thread to the egg whites. Continue whisking until cold. Whisk the egg yolks and Marsala in a double boiler, or a bowl over a pan of hot water until they thicken, then immediately remove from the heat and transfer to a cold container. Fold in the meringue mixture. If required that day, pour the zabaglione into attractive glasses and place in the refrigerator to chill, otherwise put it in a plastic container and freeze for future use.

Mela Stregata (*serves 4–6*)
Legend says that if two people drink Strega together, they will never be parted.

1pt (570ml) vanilla ice cream	2oz (55g) Menier (or similar
1tbsp (15ml) Strega liqueur (to	fine quality) chocolate
taste)	

Proceed as for any vanilla ice cream recipe. When the ice cream is cool, add the Strega and then freeze. When hard, scoop out the ice cream into balls and return these to the deep freeze to harden again.

Melt the chocolate in a double boiler, or a bowl over a pan of hot water, and quickly coat the ice cream balls, then return them to the freezer. When required, decorate with a fresh mint leaf and serve in an attractive dish. A very pleasant sauce (a little sorbet syrup plus a dash of Strega to taste) could accompany this dessert.

Meringues Glacées (*serves 6*)

FOR THE MERINGUE SHELLS:
2 egg whites
4oz (115g) caster sugar
A little caster sugar for
    sprinkling

FOR THE FILLING:
½pt (285ml) vanilla ice cream
¼pt (140ml) whipping or
    double cream
3 glacé cherries, cut in half
A little chopped angelica

As a guide, 1 egg white produces enough meringue for 6 average-sized shells. Whisk the egg whites till they stand in peaks. Slowly whisk in half the sugar (if using a machine, have it on the slowest setting at this point). Gradually fold in the remaining half of the sugar by hand, using a spatula. Line a baking tray with Bakewell paper. Using a piping bag with a plain nozzle, pipe out the meringue shells (either round or elongated). Sprinkle with caster sugar and bake very slowly in a cool oven (248°F, 120°C, Gas Mark ¼) for 3–4 hours. Remove from the paper and store in an airtight container until required.

To serve the meringues, sandwich two shells together with a scoop of vanilla ice cream and decorate with a rosette of whipped cream, topped with a glacé cherry and chopped angelica.

Pineapple Granité (*serves 10*)

A granité is simple to make, being nothing more than a frozen blend of sorbet syrup and, usually, a fruit juice. It has no meringue in it and is not churned during freezing, so it remains very granular.

1pt (570ml) sorbet syrup   1⅛pt (640ml) pineapple juice

Blend the syrup with 1pt (570ml) pineapple juice and set to freeze. Remove after 1 hour and stir the granité, but do not beat it. Repeat this after every hour. The granité should be ready in about 3–4 hours, and it will be very granular. Granités become extremely hard if left in the freezer, because of the low sugar content, so they are best eaten when just frozen. Serve in glass coupes or glasses, with the remaining pineapple juice poured over.

(*Ice cream machine*: Freeze in the churn without the paddle in place. From time to time, carefully scrape the frozen ice off the inside of the drum. Freezing should take about 25 minutes.)

Variation:
White Wine Granité
Substitute sweet white wine for the pineapple juice.

Strawberries Acapulco (*serves 2*)

The idea of having ground black pepper with fruit may seem strange. However, the husk of the pepper is sharp in flavour and is particularly good with melon or strawberries. Strawberries Acapulco is a flambé dish (brandy is added and set alight).

½oz (15g) butter	1tbsp (15ml) brandy
8oz (225g) fresh strawberries	1tbsp (15ml) double cream
Freshly ground black pepper	4 scoops vanilla ice cream

Melt the butter in a flambé pan (or small frying pan). Cut the strawberries in half and add to the butter, letting them cook for a minute. Add a couple of twists of the pepper mill, so that the resulting sauce becomes spicy. Add the brandy, heat a little, then quickly light it. Moisten with the double cream. Serve at once over the scoops of vanilla ice cream.

Strawberry Marquise (*serves 6–8*)

This dish must be served as soon as it is ready.

4oz (115g) fresh or drained, canned strawberries	½pt (285ml) whipping or double cream
1pt (570ml) cold sorbet syrup	1oz (30g) icing sugar
2tbsp (30ml) kirsch	

Liquidise the strawberries, then rub the purée through a fine sieve to remove the pips. Freeze the sorbet syrup as for a normal sorbet (see page 33). Beat in the usual way every hour. When the mixture becomes white and hardens, add the kirsch and beat it well into the mixture. Just before the marquise is required, beat the cream and icing sugar until very stiff, combine with the strawberry purée and fold into the ice mixture. Serve in delicate glasses.

ICED COUPES

Coupes are virtually sundaes, being a mixture of ice cream and fruit or sauce, and take their name from the round metal or glass dishes in which they are served. They can be accompanied by delicate sweet biscuits, such as cats' tongues, Shrewsbury cakes, etc.

Poire Belle Hélène (*serves* 6)

3 large, ripe, dessert pears
6oz (170g) granulated sugar
1pt (570ml) water
1pt (570ml) vanilla ice cream
¼pt (140ml) chocolate sauce
  (see page 81)

¼pt (140ml) whipping or
  double cream
2oz (55g) toasted flaked
  almonds

Peel the pears, cut them in half and remove the cores. Prepare a syrup with the granulated sugar and water, bring to the boil and let it bubble for 1 minute. Poach the pears in this syrup for about 10–15 minutes until not quite tender (they will continue to cook in the cooling syrup), then remove from the heat and allow to cool in the syrup.

To serve, place a large scoop of vanilla ice cream in each coupe. Cover with half a well-drained pear and then a little chocolate sauce. Pipe a rosette of whipped cream on the top and sprinkle on some toasted flaked almonds.

Variations:
The variety is unlimited. When the coupes are prepared, virtually all of them (excepting those with a hot sauce) can be decorated with a rosette of whipped cream and a sprinkling of toasted flaked almonds.

Coupe Creole
Vanilla ice cream decorated with a dice of bananas previously soaked in rum.

Coupe Danemark
Vanilla ice cream served with hot chocolate sauce.

Coupe Jacques
Vanilla ice cream and lemon ice cream decorated with a fresh fruit salad infused with lemon juice and kirsch.

Coupe Melba
Vanilla ice cream decorated with half a peach poached in syrup and coated with melba sauce (see page 82). This is often called Peach Melba.

Coupe Montmorency
Vanilla ice cream infused with kirsch and decorated with destoned cherries previously soaked in cherry brandy.

Coupe Montreuil
Peach ice cream decorated with diced fresh peaches previously soaked in kirsch.

Coupe Romanoff
Vanilla ice cream decorated with strawberries previously soaked in curaçao and sweetened to taste.

Coupe Sarah Bernhardt
Pineapple ice cream decorated with half a pear coated with a strawberry purée infused with curaçao.

Coupe Clo-Clo
Vanilla ice cream decorated with candied chestnuts which have been soaked in maraschino. Blend some whipped cream with a strawberry purée, and pipe this mixture round the border of the dish.

Coupe Petit-Duc
Vanilla Ice Cream covered with half a poached peach. Cover with a thin layer of redcurrant jam. Pipe whipped cream round the border of the dish.

ICED PANCAKES

Virtually everybody loves eating pancakes, which are usually served hot. However, iced pancakes are just the reverse – they are served only warm, with a very cold stuffing. Once the pancakes are made, the possible variations of fillings are infinite.

Basic Pancake Batter (*makes 10–12 pancakes*)

½pt (285ml) milk
2 eggs
½oz (15g) caster sugar
Pinch of salt
Grated rind of half a lemon

4oz (115g) plain flour
½oz (15g) melted butter
Oil for frying
Caster sugar for dusting

Place milk, egg, sugar, salt, and grated lemon rind in a liquidiser and switch on to maximum for 10–20 seconds. Sieve the flour and add to the liquidiser. Continue liquidising for a further 15 seconds. Switch off. If any flour remains sticking to the sides of the liquidiser, scrape it into the batter with a plastic spatula. Liquidise for a further 10 seconds, then pour the batter into a bowl. Let it rest for at least 30 minutes – the starch cells will swell and the batter will thicken.

Just before the batter is required, stir the melted butter into it. (Butter plays no part in the cooking, but adds a richness to the pancake batter.) Pancakes need a fierce heat, so heat an omelette (or crêpe) pan with a little oil until the oil smokes. Do not use butter as the frying agent – it will burn at too low a temperature. Pour off the oil into a dish and keep it for the next pancake. Hold the pan at 45 degrees and add 1 full tablespoon of batter. The batter will quickly run over the bottom of the pan. Swirl the pan around so that the pancake is paper thin. The pancake should be golden brown on the bottom within 30 seconds. Quickly turn the pancake over with a spatula and cook on the other side. Turn out on to a plate and dust with caster sugar.

Make all the pancakes in the same way and pile them up one upon the other on the plate, giving a final dusting with caster sugar. When cold, cover with foil or cling film. The pancakes will keep up to a day perfectly well in this way, though they are, of course, best eaten as soon as they are cooked.

(In a very busy professional kitchen, one chef may make up to ten or twelve pancakes at the same time, using either a griddle or a separate pan for each pancake. This demands a great deal of skill and is a sight worth seeing.)

Iced Pancakes with Maple Syrup (*serves 6*)

12 pancakes	¼pt (140ml) maple syrup
24 scoops vanilla ice cream	Toasted almonds

Warm the pancakes slightly in a non-stick frying pan with sugar and, lemon juice. Immediately fill each pancake with one ball of ice cream and fold the pancake round it into a little envelope. Put two on a plate and pour over a little maple syrup. Decorate with toasted almonds.

Variation:
Iced Chocolate Pancakes
Add 1oz (30g) cocoa powder to the batter before making the pancakes. Substitute chocolate ice cream for the vanilla. When ready to be served, coat with a little chocolate sauce (see page 81) or Crème de Cacao.

SPOOMS
Spooms are, very simply, sorbets with double the amount of meringue in them. They are therefore slightly lighter and have a little less flavour than sorbets.

Champagne Spoom (*serves 10–12*)

1pt (570ml) cold sorbet syrup	4 egg whites
1pt (570ml) champagne	8oz (225g) icing sugar

Follow the recipe for a champagne sorbet, but remember to add double the quantity of meringue, ie 4 egg whites and 8oz (225g) icing sugar.

Variations:
These are unlimited. Virtually any sorbet can be made into a spoom, but the best are those made with wine.

ICED SUNDAES
'Sundae' is a curious name for an ice cream dessert. For some obscure reason the state of Illinois did not allow ice cream sodas to be eaten on a Sunday. However, on a point of law, it was agreed that an ice cream soda was not an ice cream soda if it were served with fruit and nuts. So the new 'sundae' came into being to skirt the law, and became a great favourite.

Raspberry Sundae (*serves* 6)

1lb (450g) fresh raspberries
1pt (570ml) raspberry ice cream
2oz (55g) caster sugar
¼pt (140ml) whipping or
    double cream

2oz (55g) nib (chopped)
    almonds
6 fan wafers

Thoroughly wash and clean the raspberries. Keep back 12 raspberries for decoration, then sugar the rest. Place a large scoop of ice cream in each sundae dish and cover with the raspberries. Pipe on the whipped cream, sprinkle with nib almonds, decorate each sundae with two raspberries and finally add the wafer.

Knickerbocker Glory (*serves* 6)
Here is a real old favourite. For this dish the very tall sundae glasses will be required, plus long sundae spoons.

1 medium-sized tin of sliced
    peaches (or fruit salad)
1pt (570ml) raspery jelly
2pt (1 litre) vanilla ice cream
1pt (570ml) melba sauce (see
    page 82)
¼pt (140ml) chocolate sauce
    (see page 81)

2–3oz (55–85g) nib (chopped)
    almonds
¼pt (140ml) whipping or
    double cream
6 maraschino cherries
6 fan wafers

Chop the fruit into smallish pieces. Make the jelly and whip lightly just before it sets. Put a little fruit at the bottom of each sundae glass and cover it with a little jelly. Add a scoop of ice cream, then melba sauce. Repeat this until the top of the glass is reached, but, instead of melba sauce, add a layer of chocolate sauce. Sprinkle with the nib almonds. Pipe with a rosette of whipped cream and add a maraschino cherry and a fan wafer.

⯈ FOOLS, POSSETS, SYLLABUBS, ⯇ FLUMMERIES, FIRMITIES AND JUNKETS

FOOLS

Fools are one of the most pleasant of English sweets, taking their name from the French verb *fouler*, meaning to crush or press. They are essentially a mixture of fruit purée, sweetening and whipped cream (or a mixture of half cream and half custard instead of just cream). Virtually any non-citrus fruit can be used to make a good fool in this way.

Citrus fruits, having no pulp, require some extra ingredient to provide the bulk which is then blended with the cream. Usually this will be sponge cakes, eggs or cake crumbs. This, inevitably, masks the true flavour of the fruit, producing a fool of inferior quality to that of a non-citrus fruit.

Some fools can be frozen and served as ice cream, but in general this is not advisable unless the sugar content is high enough to stop the mixture freezing very hard.

In the past fools were slightly different from those we know today. Here is a nineteenth-century recipe for gooseberry fool, which includes an egg. The modern recipe is simpler.

Put the fruit into a stone jar, and some good sugar; set the jar on a stove or in a saucepan of water over the fire; if the former, a large spoonful of water should be added to the fruit. When it is done enough to pulp, press it through a colander; have ready a sufficient quantity of new milk, and a tea-cup of raw cream, boiled together, or an egg instead of the latter, and left to be cold; then sweeten it pretty well with sugar, and mix the pulp by degrees with it.

Gooseberry Fool (*serves 4–6*)

1½lb (680g) gooseberries
¼pt (140ml) water
6–8oz (170–225g) caster sugar

½pt (285ml) whipping or double cream

Wash, top and tail the gooseberries and poach them together with the water and sugar in a non-aluminium saucepan. (Very acidic foods tend to pit aluminium.) Do not use a lid – allow the water to evaporate and leave the cooked fruit fairly dry. When the gooseberries are very soft, after about 15–20 minutes, liquidise them, and if you wish to remove all the seeds, rub the purée through a fine sieve. As the purée cools, whip the cream until stiff, then blend the two together. Pipe into attractive glasses and chill.

All the fools can be served with ratafias, macaroons, cats' tongues, or other sweet biscuits.

Apple and Cider Fool (*serves 4–6*)

1lb (450g) cooking apples
2tbsp (30ml) sweet cider
2 pinches cinnamon
2 or 3 cloves

2–4oz (55–115g) demerara sugar
½pt (285ml) whipping or double cream

Wash the apples and cut them into quarters. Set to poach with the cider over gentle heat, together with the cinnamon, cloves and sugar. Cover with a lid. After about 10 minutes the apples will be soft enough to rub through a fine sieve, leaving the skins, core, pips and cloves behind. Cooking the apples this way (and not peeling them first) improves the flavour.

Let the purée cool. Whip the cream until stiff, and fold into the fruit purée. Pipe into attractive glasses and chill.

Blackberry Fool (*serves 4–6*)

1lb (450g) blackberries
4oz (115g) caster sugar
¼pt (140ml) water

½pt (285ml) whipping or double cream

Clean and wash the blackberries. Add the sugar to the water and poach the fruit lightly for about 5 minutes, just to soften the fruit. Strain, then rub through a fine sieve to remove the seeds. Keep the liquor on one side for future use. Whip the cream until stiff, then fold in the fruit purée. Pipe into attractive glasses and chill.

Damson Fool (*serves 4–6*)

1½lb (680g) damsons
¼pt (140ml) water
8–12oz (225–340g) granulated
  sugar

½pt (285ml) whipping or
  double cream

Damsons are extremely tart, being almost inedible in the raw state, and require a great deal of sugar. Remove any stalks or leaves, then wash the damsons and bring them to the boil in the water and sugar. Simmer for 15–20 minutes until the damsons are soft. Rub through a sieve to remove the stones and skin (keep the liquor on one side for future use). Allow to cool. Whip the cream until stiff, then fold in the damson purée. Pipe into attractive glasses and chill.

Variation:
Plum Fool
Substitute plums for the damsons.

Guava Fool (*serves 4–6*)

1lb (450g) ripe fresh guavas, or
  8oz (225g) drained, tinned
  guava flesh
Juice of half a lemon

1–2oz (30–55g) caster sugar
  (optional)
½pt (285ml) whipping or
  double cream

Peel the guavas, remove the seeds and liquidise the flesh with the lemon juice and sugar, if required. Guavas are fairly sweet, so may not need any additional sugar. Whip the cream until stiff and fold in the guava purée. Pipe into attractive glasses and chill.

Mango Fool (*serves 4–6*)
This is expensive, requiring nearly a whole ripe mango per person. It is both unusual and very delicious.

4 ripe mangoes
Juice of half a lemon

½pt (285ml) whipping or
  double cream

When ripe, the mangoes will be yellow and soft. Cut them in half, remove the flat stone and liquidise the flesh with the lemon juice. No sugar is required because ripe mangoes are very sweet indeed; the lemon is added to counteract this sweetness. Whip the cream until stiff, then fold in the mango purée. Pipe into attractive glasses and chill.

Peach Fool (*serves 4–6*)

5 ripe peaches
Juice of half a lemon

½pt (285ml) whipping or double cream

Blanch the peaches by plunging them into boiling water for about 10 seconds and then put them straight into cold water; this will loosen the skins. Cut the peaches in half, remove the skins and stones, and liquidise the flesh with the lemon juice. Whip the cream until stiff and fold in the peach purée. Pipe into attractive glasses and chill.

Prune Fool (*serves 4–6*)
Prunes make a delicious and unusual fool.

1lb (450g) prunes
1¼pt (710ml) water
2oz (55g) granulated sugar
Juice and grated rind of 1 lemon

2tbsp (30ml) port
½pt (285ml) whipping or double cream

Cover the prunes with 1pt (570ml) water and let them soak overnight. Drain off the water (as dried prunes tend to be quite dirty). Put the prunes, sugar, lemon juice and rind in a heavy-bottomed pan and bring to the boil with the remaining water. Turn down the heat and simmer slowly for about 15 minutes until the prunes are soft. Rub the prunes through a fine sieve to remove the stones. Add the port wine. Whip the cream until stiff, then fold in the prune purée. Pipe into attractive glasses and chill. The stones can be cracked open and the kernels served with the fool.

Raspberry Fool (*serves 4–6*)
Raspberries, loganberries and strawberries require no cooking.

1½lb (680g) raspberries
4–6oz (115–170g) caster sugar

½pt (285ml) whipping or double cream

Wash the raspberries and dry in a tea towel. Leave them together with the sugar in a bowl overnight. Whip the cream until stiff. Liquidise the raspberries and sugar, and fold into the cream. Pipe into attractive glasses and chill.

Rhubarb Fool (*serves 4–6*)
Rhubarb is one fruit that requires virtually no water for cooking. It must, however, be cooked very slowly in a saucepan with a tight-fitting lid, so that the steam generated from cooking condenses on the lid and turns back to water, thus aiding the cooking.

1½lb (680g) rhubarb
1tbsp (15ml) water
6–8oz (170–225g) demerara
  sugar

½pt (285ml) whipping or
  double cream
A little caster sugar to taste

Place the rhubarb, water and sugar in a heavy-bottomed pan with a tight-fitting lid. Poach the fruit very gently until soft, then liquidise it and rub the purée through a fine sieve. Allow to cool, then blend with the whipped cream. Add a little caster sugar if the mixture is too tart. Pipe into attractive glasses and chill.

POSSETS
Possets were often treated as pick-me-ups – for instance, treacle posset (milk heated and blended with treacle) was given to help cure a cold. They were also served as a hot, spiced drink at bedtime, having mainly sack, wine, beer, ale or fruit juice as a base. Another old recipe defined a posset as milk heated and served with grated bread and brandy. They were originally quite substantial, but fashions change – nowadays possets are very much lighter, being more like a syllabub but having stiffly beaten egg whites folded into the cream. Possets are enjoying a revival at the moment (like syllabubs), partly through their use in restaurants. They are delicious and easy to make – essential for the busy restaurateur who needs to make some desserts quickly!

Lemon Posset (*serves 4–6*)

2 lemons
4oz (115g) icing sugar
¼pt (140ml) dry white wine
3–4 egg whites (depending on
  how light the posset is to be)

1pt (570ml) whipping or
  double cream

Pare the rind off one of the lemons, slice the rind very thinly and reserve. Grate the rind of the other lemon. Squeeze the juice from both lemons into a bowl, adding the icing sugar, wine and grated rind. Let this stand for half an hour for the flavours to blend well. Whisk the egg whites until stiff peaks are formed. Add the cream to the wine, sugar and lemon mixture, and whisk until stiff. Fold in the egg whites very carefully. (By whisking the egg whites first, you can then use the whisks for the cream without having to wash them.) Chill well before serving and decorate with the thinly sliced lemon rind.

Variations:
Blackcurrant Posset
Substitute ¼pt (140ml) blackcurrant juice for the white wine. Add a dash of Crème de Cassis if desired.

Cherry Brandy Posset
Substitute 4tbsp (60ml) Cherry Brandy for the white wine. Decorate with a fresh cherry on each posset.

Damson Posset
Substitute ¼pt (140ml) damson wine for the white wine.

Honey and Rum Posset
Reduce the icing sugar to 3oz (85g). Substitute 2tbsp (30ml) honey and 1tbsp (15ml) rum for the white wine. This is a particularly delicious posset.

Kiwi Fruit Posset
Substitute 2 kiwi fruit for the lemons. Peel them, and save several thin slices for decoration. Liquidise the remainder, then rub them through a fine sieve. Make the posset.

Orange Posset
Substitute 2 oranges for the lemons. Decorate with thinly sliced orange rind.

SYLLABUBS

Though there are many spellings of this word (this one becoming common after 1700), they are all derived from the earlier form – sillibouk. This was a combination of silly, meaning merry and happy, and bouk, an old dialect word for belly, also a milk pail, pitcher or pot. (Bouk has become the modern word bucket.) A Derbyshire variant of this same dish is merribouk – merry, meaning happy, plus bouk. Bub is a very old slang term for a drink, as in 'our bub and our grub'. There is also a record of a silly-bub, meaning 'buttermilk mixed with newly milked sweet milk'.

Syllabub was popular in the sixteenth and seventeenth centuries and was mostly made from cider; it was the normal refreshment on a farm in late summer during harvest-time. However, there is a strong possibility that the actual practice of blending wine and milk into a drink was carried out several thousand years ago. The following two quotations (in close proximity) are from the Bible:

> I have come into my garden, my sister, my spouse: I have gathered my myrrh with my spice; I have eaten my honeycomb with my honey; I have drunk my wine with my milk: eat, O friends; drink, yea, drink abundantly, O beloved.
>
> (Solomon's Song, Chapter 5, verse 1)

> Ho, every one that thirsteth, come ye to the waters, and he that hath no money; come ye buy, and eat; yea, come, buy wine and milk without money and without price.
>
> (Isaiah, Chapter 55, Verse 1)

The modern syllabub dates from the late seventeenth and eighteenth centuries when whipped cream replaced the milk and the syllabub became more solid – much more as we know it today.

Fruit syllabubs are very similar to fools but have the additional ingredient of wine. They are particularly pleasant in summer. All syllabubs should be served chilled and accompanied by sweet biscuits.

Banana Syllabub (*serves 4–6*)

4 large bananas
Juice of half a lemon
1pt (570ml) whipping or
   double cream
2oz (55g) caster sugar

2tbsp (30ml) white wine

TO DECORATE:
Thinly sliced rind of half
   a lemon

Peel the bananas and liquidise them with the lemon juice. Put into a bowl, together with the cream, sugar and wine. Beat until the cream starts to thicken. Pipe into tulip-shaped glasses and chill. Decorate with the thinly sliced lemon rind.

Champagne Syllabub (*serves 4–6*)

Half a lemon
2oz (55g) caster sugar
¼pt (140ml) champagne (pink champagne is excellent)
1pt (570ml) whipping or double cream

TO DECORATE:
A few black grapes

Grate the lemon rind and extract the juice. Put into a bowl with the sugar and champagne. Leave for an hour for the flavours to mingle. Strain, then add the cream. Beat until the cream starts to thicken. Pipe into tulip-shaped glasses and chill. Decorate with de-pipped black grapes.

Damson Syllabub (*serves 4–6*)
This syllabub has a delightful pale pink colour

1 small lemon
2oz (55g) caster sugar
¼pt (140ml) damson wine
1pt (570ml) whipping or double cream

TO DECORATE:
Toasted flaked almonds

Grate half the rind and extract the juice from the lemon. Put into a bowl with the sugar and damson wine. Leave for an hour for the flavours to mingle. Strain, then add cream. Beat until the cream begins to thicken. Pipe into tulip-shaped glasses and chill. Decorate with toasted flaked almonds.

Variations:
Plum Syllabub
Substitute plum juice for the damson wine.

Prune Syllabub
Liquidise ¼pt (140ml) destoned prunes in their juice. Rub the purée through a fine sieve. Substitute this prune purée for the damson wine.

Lemon Syllabub (*serves 4–6*)

1 large lemon
2oz (55g) caster sugar
2tbsp (30ml) white wine

1pt (570ml) whipping or
    double cream

Remove the rind of the lemon. Slice half very thinly and grate the remainder. Extract the juice from the lemon and put into a bowl with the sugar, grated rind and wine. Leave for an hour for the flavours to mingle. Strain the liquid into a clean bowl, then add the cream. Beat slowly until the cream starts to thicken. Pipe into tulip-shaped glasses and chill. Decorate the top of each syllabub with the thinly sliced lemon rind.

Praline Syllabub (*serves 4–6*)

2oz (55g) flaked almonds
1oz (30g) granulated sugar
Half a lemon
2oz (55g) caster sugar

2tbsp (30ml) white wine
1pt (570ml) whipping or
    double cream

Make the praline as described on page 87. Grate the lemon rind and extract the juice. Put into a bowl with the sugar and wine. Leave for an hour for the flavours to mingle. Strain, then add the cream and three-quarters of the praline mixture. Beat until the cream starts to thicken. Pipe into tulip-shaped glasses and chill. Sprinkle the remaining praline on top for decoration.

Raspberry Syllabub (*serves 4–6*)

8oz (225g) fresh raspberries
Juice of half a lemon
2oz (55g) caster sugar
2tbsp (30ml) white wine
1pt (570ml) whipping or
    double cream

TO DECORATE:
6 fresh mint leaves
6 raspberries

Liquidise the raspberries and rub the purée through a fine sieve to remove any pips. Put the lemon juice, sugar and wine in a bowl. Leave for an hour for the flavours to mingle. Strain the liquid into a clean bowl, then add the cream and raspberry purée. Beat slowly until the cream starts to thicken. Pipe into tulip-shaped glasses and chill. Decorate the top of each syllabub with a fresh mint leaf and a raspberry.

Staffordshire Syllabub

This and the following two recipes are taken from *A New System of Domestic Cookery, by a Lady* (Mrs Rundell) published in 1828. They show very clearly how syllabubs have changed over the years.

'Put a pint of cider, and a glass of brandy, sugar and nutmeg, into a bowl, and milk into it; or pour warm milk from a large tea pot some height into it.'

A syllabub was made with milk drawn directly from the cow into the wine, hence it became frothy. If no cow was available the action of pouring from some height created the froth.

A Very Fine Somersetshire and Devon Syllabub

'In a very large China bowl put a pint of port, and a pint of sherry or other white wine; sugar to taste. Milk the bowl full. In twenty minutes time cover it pretty high with clouted cream; grate over it nutmeg, put pounded cinnamon, and nonpareil comfits.'

Clouted cream is not clotted cream as we know it today but a specific preparation (see recipe which follows). As regards 'nonpareil comfits', comfits are preserved fruits and nonpareil (when applied to fruits) means of matchless or unsurpassed quality.

Clouted Cream

'String four blades of mace on a thread; put them to a gill of new milk, and six spoonsful of rose water; simmer a few minutes; then by degrees stir this liquor strained into the yolks of two new eggs well beaten. Stir the whole into a quart of very good cream, and set it over the fire; stir it till hot, but not boiling hot; pour it into a deep dish, and let it stand twenty-four hours. Serve it in a cream dish to eat with fruits. Many people prefer it without any flavour but that of cream; in which case use a quart of new milk and the cream, or do it as the Devonshire scalded cream.

When done enough, a round mark will appear on the surface of the cream, the size of the bottom of the pan it is done in, which in the country they call the ring; and when that is seen, remove the pan from the fire.'

FLUMMERIES AND FIRMITIES

The curiously named flummery is a very old dish. The name is derived from the Welsh 'llymry', meaning wash-brew, and 'llym', sour or sharp. Flummeries have undergone a great change over the years. The original flummery was made by soaking oatmeal in water for a day and a half to two days. The whole was then strained through a hair sieve and boiled till thick as 'hasty pudding'. During Tudor and Stuart times, flummery became a much richer dish of cream with the addition of sugar and orange-flowered water. This was allowed to set in a shallow dish or elaborate mould and eaten in the second course with cream or wine poured over it.

Several hundred years ago flummeries were much more popular than they are today. For elaborate banquets, for instance, they were often set in highly ornate moulds, becoming the centre-piece of a table display. Flummeries are still best made in such moulds (if the moulds can be found!), but nowadays they are set with gelatine.

Dutch Flummery (serves 6–8)

1oz (30g) gelatine
3oz (85g) caster sugar
Rind and juice of 1 lemon
1pt (570ml) sherry

1pt (570ml) water
4 eggs
1 egg yolk

TO DECORATE:
A little whipping or double cream

Combine all the ingredients, except the eggs, and heat gently in the top of a double boiler or bowl over a pan of hot water until the sugar and gelatine have dissolved. Whisk the eggs and yolk to a mousse and add to the mixture. Stir briskly until the mixture thickens, then pour it into a mould rinsed with cold water (so that the flummery will turn out easily). Allow to cool before putting it into the refrigerator to set. Turn out from the mould and decorate with piped rosettes of cream.

English Flummery (*serves 4–6*)

1oz (30g) gelatine
1pt (570ml) whipping or
  double cream
Grated rind and juice of
  1 orange

3oz (85g) caster sugar

TO DECORATE:
A little whipping or double
  cream

Combine all the ingredients and heat gently in the top of a double boiler or bowl over a pan of hot water until the sugar and gelatine have dissolved. Rinse a mould with cold water, then pour the mixture into the mould and leave to cool before putting it into the refrigerator to set. Turn out from the mould and decorate with piped rosettes of cream. (A very old accompaniment for this dish is baked pears – though I have never found these to be too popular!)

Somersetshire Firmity

Firmities were often prepared in invalid cookery but, unlike flummeries, are not seen nowadays. The following recipe is taken from *A New System of Domestic Cookery, by a Lady* (Mrs Rundell) published in 1828.

'To a quart of ready boiled wheat, put by degrees two quarts of new milk, breaking the jelly, and then four ounces of currants, picked clean, and washed; stir them and boil till they are done. Beat the yolks of three eggs, and a little nutmeg, with two or three spoonsful of milk; add this to the wheat; stir them together while over the fire; then sweeten, and serve cold in a deep dish. Some persons like it best warm.'

JUNKET

Milk has always been prominent in our diets. Junket is a very old English dish, and is, very probably, the simplest of milk puddings to make. The curious name is based on the Latin word *juncus*, meaning rush, and the old French word *jonquette*, meaning a rush basket, in which the junkets were made.

In making a junket, the milk is curdled by the addition of rennet (from the Old English 'rinnan', meaning to run together, or coagulate) which is an extract from the lining of a calf's stomach. This coagulates the milk and sets it. Junkets were often flavoured with spices and were served alongside the flummeries at feasts. The word 'junketing' also meant 'making merry, and feasting'. The modern junket, rarely eaten these days, is less elaborate and

78

extremely simple to make. However, the milk must be no hotter than blood heat (98.4°F, 36.8°C) in order for the enzyme in rennet to coagulate it. Furthermore, it must be fresh or pasteurised – rennet will not work with boiled or sterilised milk.

Caramel Junket (*serves 4*)

2oz (55g) granulated sugar	TO DECORATE:
1tbsp (15ml) water	¼pt (140ml) whipping or
1pt (570ml) milk	double cream
1tsp (5ml) rennet	1oz (30g) toasted flaked
	almonds

Heat the sugar in a heavy-bottomed pan until the caramel stage is reached. Very carefully cool it with a few drops of water. Add the 1tbsp (15ml) water to the caramel and stir in. Leave to cool.

Heat the milk very gently in the same pan with the caramel until blood heat is reached. Add the rennet and stir well in. Pour into attractive glasses and leave to set in a warm place for 3–4 hours. Place in the refrigerator when the junket is quite firm. Decorate with rosettes of whipped cream and toasted flaked almonds.

Note: If the dish is required in a hurry, use double the quantity of rennet and reduce the setting time to 1½ hours.

Variations:
Coffee Junket
Omit the water. Add 2tsp (10ml) coffee essence or instant coffee to the milk and heat with the sugar to blood heat. Stir in the rennet. Leave to set, and decorate as for caramel junket.

Rum Junket
Omit the water. Add 2tbsp (30ml) dark rum to the milk and heat with the sugar to blood heat. Stir in the rennet. Leave to set, and decorate as for caramel junket.

Plain Junket with Nutmeg
Omit the water. Heat the milk to blood heat. Stir in the rennet. Leave to set. Grate a little nutmeg on the top. Decorate as for a caramel junket or serve simply with clotted cream.

≫ACCOMPANYING SWEET SAUCES, ≪ BISCUITS AND SUNDRIES

SWEET SAUCES

Accompanying sauces really do improve a dessert; indeed, for most children, the topping is actually more important than the ice cream being served.

Cardinal Sauce (*makes about ¾pt [430ml]*)

4oz (115g) raspberries	¼pt (140ml) water
4oz (115g) strawberries	4oz (115g) caster sugar
1tsp (5ml) custard powder	

Liquidise the soft fruit. Mix the custard powder with 1tbsp (15ml) water. Bring the soft fruit to the boil in a heavy-bottomed pan together with the sugar and the remainder of the water. Skim, then add the custard powder. Continue cooking for a minute, then strain and leave to cool.

Cold Butterscotch Sauce (*makes about ½pt [285ml]*)

1oz (30g) butter	5oz (140g) soft brown sugar
2 level tbsp (30ml) golden syrup	¼pt (140ml) single cream

Melt the butter, golden syrup and sugar. Bring to the boil. When the sugar is liquid, stir in the cream. Reheat again. Strain into a bowl. Very often grains of sugar remain unmelted, and it is a pity to leave them in the sauce as it will then become granular.

Variation:
Cold Butterscotch and Nut Sauce
Add 1oz (30g) praline powder (see page 87) to the sauce. Alternatively, add 1oz (30g) roughly chopped walnuts or ground hazelnuts.

Chocolate Sauce (*makes about ½pt [285ml]*)

3½oz (100g) Menier (or similar   ¼pt (140ml) whipping or
  fine quality) chocolate   double cream
4tbsp (60ml) water   1oz (30g) butter

Melt the chocolate with the water in a heavy-bottomed pan (or double boiler) over gentle heat. Stir until all the chocolate has melted, then add the cream and butter. Continue heating till the cream and butter are well blended. Whisk quickly for a minute. Serve either hot or cold. This sauce will keep in the refrigerator for 3–4 days.

(For those with a microwave oven, put the chocolate and water into a plastic or glass bowl. Place in the microwave oven and set for 1½ minutes. Remove, add the cream and butter, and stir well. The sauce can be prepared very quickly in this way.)

Variation:
Chocolate Peppermint Sauce
Add 2–3 drops peppermint essence to the above recipe. (If peppermint essence proves difficult to obtain, good chemists usually stock it or they might be prepared to order some for you.)

Fruit Sauce (*makes about 1½pt [855ml]*)
Suitable for any pulp fruit, such as peaches, strawberries, raspberries, apricots, etc.

1lb (450g) fruit jam   Juice of half a lemon
½pt (285ml) water   2tbsp (30ml) kirsch

Bring the jam, water and lemon juice to the boil in a heavy-bottomed pan. Simmer for 3 minutes. Skim, if necessary, then liquidise and strain. Add the kirsch. Allow to cool, and serve cold.

Honey and Whisky Sauce

¼pt (140ml) whipping or   ¼pt (140ml) honey
  double cream   2tbsp (30ml) whisky

Heat the cream and honey in a double boiler over gentle heat. Add the whisky and blend well together. This is best served hot (and especially good in the winter!).

Hot Chocolate Fudge Sauce

1oz (30g) demerara sugar
3½oz (100g) Menier (or similar
  fine quality) plain chocolate
3tbsp (45ml) water

¼pt (140ml) condensed milk
1oz (30g) butter

Melt the sugar in the water in a pan over gentle heat. Add the remaining ingredients and stir well together. Serve hot.

Jubilee Sauce (*makes about ¾pt [430ml]*)
This is a much simpler version of the recipe on page 56.

1 × 14oz (395g) can pitted
  black cherries

1tsp (5ml) arrowroot
1tbsp (15ml) kirsch

Drain the cherries. Blend the arrowroot with 1tbsp (15ml) cherry juice. Bring the remainder of the juice to the boil. Add the arrowroot and juice mixture, and continue cooking till the cherry juice clears and starts to thicken. Remove from the heat and strain. Add the kirsch, and drained cherries. This sauce can be served hot or cold.

Melba Sauce (*makes about ¼pt [140ml]*)
This sauce is usually used for a Coupe Melba, and the raspberries are not cooked, merely puréed.

2oz (55g) granulated sugar
1tbsp (15ml) water

Juice of 1 lemon
4oz (115g) fresh raspberries

Boil the sugar, water and lemon juice together for 1 minute. When cold, liquidise with the raspberries. Strain to remove the pips.

Rum Sauce (*makes about ½pt [285ml]*)

1oz (30g) butter
2 level tbsp (30ml) golden syrup

4oz (115g) soft brown sugar
6tbsp (90ml) dark rum

Melt the butter, golden syrup and sugar. Bring to the boil. When the sugar is liquid, remove from the heat and stir in the rum. Strain into a bowl. This sauce can be served hot or cold.

Variation:
Rum and Honey Sauce
Prepare as above, but use 3oz (85g) soft brown sugar and 2tbsp (30ml) honey. This is a very good sauce.

BISCUITS

These are best eaten fresh from the oven, as biscuits absorb moisture from the air and so become soft. However, if they are placed in an airtight container as soon as they are cool, they will stay crisp for 2–3 days. They can also be 'recrisped' in the oven if they do become soft.

Brunswick Biscuits (*makes about 24–28 individual biscuits*)

These have a delicious spicy flavour. They can be sandwiched as in the recipe, or eaten on their own.

8oz (225g) plain flour
2 level tsp (10ml) ground
  cinnamon
Pinch of salt
1 level tsp (5ml) baking powder
4oz (115g) butter
4oz (115g) caster sugar
1 beaten egg

FOR THE ICING:
4tbsp (60ml) raspberry jam
1tbsp (15ml) water
4oz (115g) sifted icing sugar
1–2 drops pink food colouring
6–7 glacé cherries, cut in half

Very lightly grease two baking trays. Sift together the flour, cinnamon, salt and baking powder. Cream the butter until soft and light, then beat in the caster sugar. Add the beaten egg, working it well into the mixture, then add the flour. Roll the mixture thinly and, using a 3in (7.5cm) plain cutter, cut out the biscuits, laying them on the prepared baking trays. Bake in a moderate oven (350°F, 180°C, Gas Mark 4) for 15–20 minutes. Remove and lay on a wire rack to cool.

When cold, sandwich two biscuits together with a layer of raspberry jam. Add the water to the icing sugar and mix well together. Add the colouring (if used). Spread the icing on top of each double biscuit and put half a glacé cherry in the middle. Alternatively, the plain biscuits can be stored in an airtight container and iced when required.

Cats' Tongues (*makes about 40*)

This recipe is based on the one I used when working abroad. In a professional kitchen, the ovens are on most of the time the kitchen is in use, and these biscuits can be cooked quickly in an oven which is at the right temperature. However, in the home it would be expensive to put on the oven just to cook some cats' tongues, so they are best done when other baking is required.

¼pt (140ml) double cream
7oz (200g) caster sugar
1–2 drops vanilla essence

8oz (225g) sifted plain flour
6 egg whites

Whip the cream until stiff, add the sugar and vanilla essence, then fold in the sifted flour. Whisk the egg whites till stiff and fold them into the mixture. Lightly grease a baking tray. Using a plain ½in (1cm) nozzle in a piping bag, pipe the mixture on to the baking tray in 3in (7.5cm) lengths, remembering to leave at least 1in (2.5cm) between each cats' tongue to allow for spreading during cooking. Bake in a hot oven (425°F, 220°C, Gas Mark 7) for about 8 minutes until golden with a tinge of brown round the edges. Remove from the baking tray and leave to cool on a wire rack. When cold, store in an airtight container.

Digestive Biscuits (*makes about 20*)

1oz (30g) oatmeal
6oz (170g) wholemeal flour
1oz (30g) white flour
2oz (55g) caster sugar

1tsp (5ml) baking powder
3oz (85g) soft butter
⅛pt (70ml) milk

Mix all the dry ingredients and thoroughly rub in the soft butter. Using a mixer, gradually add the milk till a soft dough is obtained. Remove from the bowl and roll out very thinly on a floured board. Using a 3in (7.5cm) plain cutter, cut out the biscuits and place them on an ungreased tray. Bake in a moderate oven (350°F, 180°C, Gas Mark 4) for about 20 minutes, when the biscuits will be crisp. Remove from the oven and leave to cool on a wire rack. When completely cold, store in an airtight container.

Ratafias (*makes about 40*)

3 egg whites
8oz (225g) ground almonds

12oz (340g) caster sugar

Thoroughly mix all the ingredients together. Line two baking sheets with rice paper. Roll out very small balls of the mixture with the hands and place these 1in (2.5cm) apart on the prepared baking sheets. Alternatively, if a large quantity is being cooked, pipe out ½in (1cm) rounds, using a piping bag with a very small plain nozzle. Again, leave at least 1in (2.5cm) between ratafias. Bake in a cool oven (300°F, 150°C, Gas Mark 2) for about 25 minutes, until light brown. Leave to cool on a wire rack. When completely cold, store in an airtight container.

Shortbread Fingers (*makes 24*)
An excellent accompaniment for ice cream. Care must be taken in the cooking so that the finished shortbread melts in the mouth and does not become chewy. The secret lies in a long, slow baking at a low temperature.

1lb (450g) plain flour	4oz (115g) caster sugar
10oz (280g) butter	A little caster sugar for dredging

Thoroughly sift the flour. Cream the butter and sugar until white, then gradually work in the flour. Press into two 8 × 12in (20 × 30cm) Swiss roll tins, then prick with a fork. Bake in a cool oven (300°F, 150°C, Gas Mark 2) for about 1 hour. Remove from the oven, cut into fingers whilst still warm, then dredge with caster sugar. Cool on a wire rack. When completely cold, store in an airtight container.

Shrewsbury Biscuits (*makes 20*)

6oz (170g) plain flour	4oz (115g) caster sugar
Pinch of salt	1tsp (5ml) ground mace
4oz (115g) unsalted butter	1 egg

Thoroughly sift the flour and salt. Cream the butter. Mix the sugar and mace, and gradually beat into the butter. Add the egg and mix well, then add the sifted flour. Line two baking trays with grease-proof paper or Bakewell paper. Roll out the dough thinly, and cut into rounds with a 3in (7.5cm) cutter. Place the biscuits on the lined baking trays. Bake in a moderate oven (350°F, 180°C, Gas Mark 4) for 12–15 minutes, until lightly golden at the edges. Cool on a wire rack. When completely cold, store in an airtight container.

Sponge Fingers (*makes about 24*)

3oz (85g) plain flour   3oz (85g) caster sugar
3 eggs   A little caster sugar for dusting

Set the oven to moderately hot (375°F, 190°C, Gas Mark 5). Prepare two baking trays, lining them with either greaseproof paper or Bakewell paper. Thoroughly sift the flour. Separate the eggs into yolks and whites. Whisk the yolks with half the sugar till thick and moussy. Beat the whites till stiff, then carefully add the remaining half of the sugar – this is to give them more body as, in general, beaten egg whites do not readily blend with whisked egg yolks. Very gently, but as quickly as possible, combine the egg whites with the yolks, then fold in the sifted flour. If there is too much delay before mixing the whites with the yolks, the mixture will become grainy and cook in an irregular fashion.

Using a piping bag with a plain ½in (1cm) nozzle, pipe out the fingers in 3in (7.5cm) lengths on the prepared, lined baking trays. Dust with the caster sugar (tipping off the residue which can be used again). Cook near the top of the preheated oven for about 8–10 minutes, until the fingers are a very light brown. Leave to cool on a wire rack. When completely cold, store in an airtight container.

Sweet Oat Biscuits (*makes about 28*)
These are extremely useful, as they can be eaten by those people on a gluten-free diet.

¼oz (7g) margarine   A pinch of bicarbonate of soda
⅛pt (70ml) hot water   2oz (55g) caster sugar
4oz (115g) oatmeal

Melt the margarine in the hot water. Place the oatmeal in a food mixer together with the bicarbonate of soda and sugar. Run the mixer on half speed, gradually adding the water and margarine mixture. When all the water is added, turn the speed up to full and continue for a minute until the dough has become moist and smooth. Turn off the mixer. Dust the rolling pin and pastry board with oatmeal and roll out the dough as thinly as possible:

Using a 2in (5cm) plain or fluted cutter, cut out the biscuits and place them on an ungreased tray. Bake in a moderate oven (350°F, 180°C, Gas Mark 4) for about 20 minutes, when the biscuits will be crisp and just turning a golden colour. Remove from the oven and leave to cool on a wire rack. When completely cold, store in an airtight container.

SUNDRIES
Caraque Chocolate

2oz (55g) Menier (or similar fine quality) chocolate

Carefully melt the chocolate in a double boiler (or a bowl over a pan of hot water). Whilst still warm, use a palette knife to spread it very thinly on a cold surface, such as a marble slab. As soon as it cools, scrape the chocolate up into curls with a sharp knife. These look most attractive as decorations. If not wanted immediately, cover and store in a cool place.

Praline

3½oz (100g) caster sugar
3½oz (100g) flaked almonds or crushed hazelnuts

Lightly oil a baking tray. Heat the caster sugar and nuts in a thick-bottomed pan. Stir with a metal spoon until the caramel stage is reached, then quickly pour this mixture on to the baking tray. Let it cool. When the mixture has set hard, break it up into small pieces and grind these to a fine powder in a blender or food processor.

This mixture is best used as soon as it is made. If it is kept, it tends to absorb moisture very quickly and becomes soft.

≫ APPENDIX ≪

FROZEN YOGHURTS

These unusual recipes have been included because light, frozen, savoury starters are becoming popular. They are not sorbets, and are best eaten when freshly made. If kept, they will become solid in the deep freeze (for they contain little, if any, sugar) and will require ripening again before they can be served. A liquidiser or food processor is needed.

Note Whipped sour cream may be used in place of the yoghurt in these recipes.

Iced Avocado and Cheese Yoghurt (*serves 6*)

1 clove garlic, peeled
Pinch of salt
2 ripe avocado pears
1 medium cucumber
2 egg whites
4tbsp (60ml) ready-made
    mayonnaise

4tbsp (60ml) plain yoghurt
Juice of 1 lemon
4oz (115g) soft cheese
1–2 drops Worcestershire sauce
1–2 twists of the peppermill

Sprinkle the garlic with a little salt and crush it to a purée with the flat of a knife blade. The salt is abrasive and breaks up the tissues. Remove the stones from the avocado pears and scoop out the flesh; keep the skin for serving. Peel and de-pip the cucumber, saving a little peel for garnishing. Whisk the egg whites until stiff. Blend all the ingredients together in the liquidiser. Set to freeze. This will take about 3 hours.

Serve the iced yoghurt, which is a beautiful, very pale green, in the avocado skins decorated with very thinly sliced cucumber peel. A fresh sprig of watercress or black olives could also be added for colour.

(*Ice cream machine:* Place the purée in the freezing churn. This mixture is ready in 15–20 minutes.)

Tomato Sorbet (serves 4–6)

1lb (450g) ripe tomatoes
1 clove garlic, peeled
Pinch of salt
2 egg whites
¼pt (140ml) plain yoghurt

1–2 drops Worcestershire sauce
1oz (30g) tomato purée
1 pinch fresh thyme
1–2 twists of the peppermill

Blanch the tomatoes for 10 seconds in boiling water, then remove the skins and seeds. Crush the garlic with the salt to a fine purée. Whisk the egg whites until stiff. Place all the ingredients in the blender and liquidise them thoroughly. Set to freeze. This will take about 3 hours.

(*Ice cream machine:* Place the mixture in the freezing churn. It will be ready in about 15–20 minutes.)

12 *Advertisements.*

SPECIMENS FROM
THE BOOK OF MOULDS
Containing 68 pages of Illustrations, published by
MARSHALL'S SCHOOL OF COOKERY
And sent POST FREE on application.

FANCY ICE MOULDS IN PEWTER.

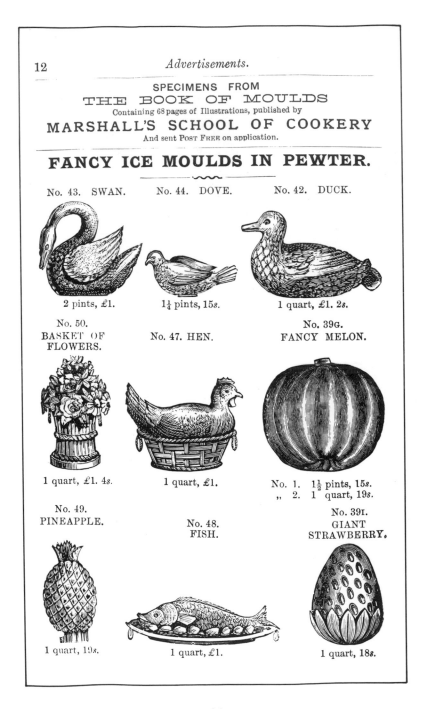

No. 43. SWAN.　　No. 44. DOVE.　　No. 42. DUCK.

2 pints, £1.　　1¼ pints, 15s.　　1 quart, £1. 2s.

No. 50.
BASKET OF
FLOWERS.　　No. 47. HEN.

No. 39G.
FANCY MELON.

1 quart, £1. 4s.　　1 quart, £1.

No. 1.　1½ pints, 15s.
„ 2.　1 quart, 19s.

No. 49.
PINEAPPLE.

No. 48.
FISH.

No. 39I.
GIANT
STRAWBERRY.

1 quart, 19s.　　1 quart, £1.　　1 quart, 18s.

90

≫ GLOSSARY ≪

Bakewell paper A cooking parchment with non-stick properties. It is extremely useful in pastry work, and can also be used for inter-leaving in a freezer.

To blanch The method of dipping food (such as tomatoes or peaches) into boiling water for a matter of seconds to make peeling easier.

Blood heat 94.4°F, 36.8°C.

Caramel stage The point at which sugar turns a light golden brown (356°F, 180°C).

Corn syrup A syrup made from corn starch. It varies in colour from clear to amber and is used in the production of glucose and confectionery.

To fold in To combine mixtures, such as whipped egg whites or whipped cream, so that lightness is not lost.

Pitted Destoned; usually referring to fruit such as cherries.

To purée To liquidise fruit or pass it through a sieve.

Rice paper An edible paper made from potato flour, rice flour and an oil. It is extremely useful in pastry making.

Ripening (of ice creams) Softening ice cream in the main compart-ment of a refrigerator prior to serving (see Introduction).

Rosette (of cream) Whipped cream piped through a star-shaped nozzle so that the cream forms a rosette shape.

Saccharometer A specialised hydrometer for measuring the density of a sugar syrup (see Introduction).

Stabiliser An ingredient, often gelatine, added to a mixture to help bind all the other ingredients together (see Introduction).

Sugar syrup A solution of sugar in water. The ratio of sugar to water is usually measured in degrees – thus a 12° syrup (required for a granité) contains less sugar than an 18–22° syrup (required for a fruit ice cream). Too much sugar and the ice will not freeze, too little and it will freeze hard (see Introduction).

Sugar thermometer A thermometer for measuring sugar boiling (see Introduction).

≫ INDEX ≪